Behaviour in the Early Years

This accessible and practical book provides hands-on, tried and tested strategies to help the reader respond instantly and effectively to behaviour problems in early years settings. It encourages the practitioner to think about how they handle difficult situations and to understand why children behave as they do.

Including topics on the development of the child from birth to toddler, managing the environment, and safeguarding children, this third edition has also been fully updated to include:

- guidance on complex learning difficulties, including autism and speech and language disorders;
- exploration of the use and impact of social media, technology and digital devices on social interaction;
- managing and facilitating the transition from an early years setting to school;
- an outline of the Education and Health Care Plan, including request and implementation.

Other features include a vast number of case studies, social and developmental checklists, a glossary and useful addresses.

With ideas and strategies that can easily be absorbed into the daily routine, this book is essential reading for practitioners in all early years settings looking for effective ways to deal with challenging behaviour.

Angela Glenn is a recently retired advisory teacher for Medway Education Authority.

Jacquie Cousins is a freelance educational consultant.

Alicia Helps was an educational psychologist.

Behaviour in the Early Years

Third Edition

Angela Glenn,
Jacquie Cousins and
Alicia Helps

Routledge
Taylor & Francis Group

LONDON AND NEW YORK

Third edition published 2019
by Routledge
2 Park Square, Milton Park, Abingdon, Oxon, OX14 4RN

and by Routledge
711 Third Avenue, New York, NY 10017

Routledge is an imprint of the Taylor & Francis Group, an informa business

© 2019 Angela Glenn, Jacquie Cousins and Alicia Helps

First edition published by David Fulton Publishers 2006
Second edition published by Routledge 2011

British Library Cataloguing in Publication Data
A catalogue record for this book is available from the British Library

Library of Congress Cataloging in Publication Data
Names: Glenn, Angela, author. | Cousins, Jacquie, author. | Helps, Alicia, author.
Title: Behaviour in the early years / Angela Glenn, Jacquie Cousins and
    Alicia Helps.Other titles: Behavior in the early years
Description: Third edition. | Abingdon, Oxon ; New York, NY : Routledge, 2019.
Identifiers: LCCN 2018025195 (print) | LCCN 2018036316 (ebook) |
    ISBN 9781315121222 (ebook) | ISBN 9781138562318 (hardback) |
    ISBN 9781138562325 (pbk.) | ISBN 9781315121222 (ebk.)
Subjects: LCSH: Problem children—Education (Preschool)—England—
    Medway. | Education, Preschool—England—Medway.
Classification: LCC LC4803.G72 (ebook) | LCC LC4803.G72 M433 2018
    (print) | DDC 370.15/28—dc23
LC record available at https://lccn.loc.gov/2018025195

ISBN: 978-1-138-56231-8 (hbk)
ISBN: 978-1-138-56232-5 (pbk)
ISBN: 978-1-315-12122-2 (ebk)

Typeset in Times New Roman
by Swales & Willis Ltd, Exeter, Devon, UK

CONTENTS

ACKNOWLEDGEMENTS

We would like to thank Sarah Glenn, Eden Lily Howells, Isabella Rose Whitehead and Gabriel Ahmad for providing the illustrations. We would also like to thank Simon Hughes for his help.

In memory of our friend and colleague Alicia who is greatly missed.

INTRODUCTION

This book was written in response to requests for advice from practitioners working with young children across a range of early years settings. Experience in delivering in-service training sessions and professional development courses has shown us that colleagues are looking for straightforward guidance in dealing with the challenges presented by many of the children they meet – particularly in matters concerning behaviour. We would like to stress that this is not a text book about child development, psychology or other issues (for example, anxiety and separation disorders). Indeed, although these particular issues may have a significant impact upon behaviour, we have tried to keep things simple by describing behaviours and giving some ideas about how to support children. This book is meant to provide an accessible handbook for the early years practitioner when faced with behaviours that are causing concern. Whenever intervening to support children's behaviour, a rounded view of their development will help, and important issues like attachment, separation and environmental factors must be taken into account. However, the intention here is not to dismiss the importance of serious subjects like anxiety and others mentioned above but rather, to provide some ideas about how to address immediate concerns. This book is intended to be a practical guide to help practitioners plan, support and manage children's behaviour. Considered, sensitive, early intervention can be key.

I'm tired and I don't want to put my bricks away. I miss my mummy and I want to go home.

We have put together a range of common situations and suggested some 'tried and tested' approaches. There is no magic wand and these simple approaches will not always work. There will be children whose needs are more complex and who therefore need more expert intervention. The strategies suggested should not be seen as 'one size fits all' but rather as a guide for intervention, support and management. It should be remembered that 'typical' development spans a wide range and that every child develops along a unique pathway. The best course of action is only to intervene when and if it is necessary.

However, the majority of children will respond to consistent, 'firm but fair' handling with lots of praise and positive reinforcement.

As will be seen from the examples given, it can sometimes be very difficult to be clear about the causes of children's difficulties but we do know the child is trying to tell us something through their behaviour. Young children do not have the verbal skills of an adult and therefore we need to be sensitive to what it is that the child is attempting to communicate. This is easier said than done when the child is behaving in a challenging manner. We hope this book will be one way of helping practitioners to understand what the child is trying to communicate as well as providing some practical ideas to deal with difficult situations.

It can be difficult for professionals to provide with any accuracy a 'diagnosis' for a child at the pre-school stage. It is not always possible to differentiate between the child who has neurological difficulties such as Autistic Spectrum Disorder (ASD) and the child who has symptoms of anxiety caused by emotional distress. Both children may develop repetitive and immature behaviour that makes them feel more secure and both could present as being withdrawn and not responding to instructions. When a referral to a specialist professional is made it will be very useful if the practitioner concerned can offer accurate observations and details of the strategies that have/have not been successful. The pre-school practitioner can provide very useful information in advising professionals about social, cognitive and emotional aspects of the child's functioning.

This third edition of our book will cover the following new additions:

- A new section on more specific conditions that can result in behavioural issues, such as ASD and speech and language disorders.
- A new section on the use of technology in early years settings.
- An updated section on safeguarding.
- A new section on moving on to school and transitional issues.
- A new section on the changes to the Code of Practice and a brief description of the Education and Health Care Plan and the implications for early years settings.

From birth to toddler

Step 1: Be consistent

Step 2: Use praise and rewards

Step 3: Provide good models

Step 4: Guide the child

Step 5: Ignore bad behaviour

Step 6: Remove from the scene

Step 7: Apply sanctions

Some additional ideas

The birth of a newborn baby is usually a joyous event and that baby is usually born into a family that includes many relations and also a network of friends, each with their own ideas on child rearing.

The first few months will be a time of adapting to a new family member who will very soon establish a personality of her own. Most babies go through a separation anxiety stage at about nine months where they may become very anxious when away from the main carer(s). Babies have emotions and needs from birth and initially express them through crying, but gradually babies gain increasing mobility by initially crawling or rolling and can go and reach out for things and go to things themselves. At this stage the main aim is to think about hygiene and safety for baby.

Gradually as babies become more mobile they become more independent and are more exploratory. This exploration can lead to problems and is the essential stage where parents or carers need to be very cautious and make clear to the child what they can and what they can't do. A firm, low voice usually works well. Although some of the antics seem funny, it is important not to laugh, as the child will think this is a game and will carry on with the game as long as possible. This would eventually result in the adult becoming very frustrated and very annoyed, sending a very mixed message to the child. Gradually as the child becomes more aware of his environment, the type of behaviour can continue when the child knows it can get a response. It can be at this early stage that parents can begin to feel demoralized so that they are unable to manage their child.

This is also the stage when children want to do more but need more adult help and demand it more if they don't get the support needed. From about 18 months, as mobility increases, toddlers form stronger ideas about likes and dislikes, often acquiring very strong wills. This is the stage of the 'terrible twos' as it is often called. When a toddler wants something she wants it instantly and can feel that others are preventing her from getting it. At this stage the child will not have developed sufficient self control in order for an adult to be able to negotiate with her. Parents can imagine that a child who is able to speak is also able to understand. This is where difficulties arise, as parents may try to reason with a child who has not sufficiently developed emotionally to deal with the frustrations she is feeling. This is certainly a challenging time for parents and carers, as stroppiness and inability to reason often leads to tantrums.

Remember the 3 C's – be clear, concise and calm

- Be clear in what you say and focus on one aspect at a time.
- Be very concise and use as few words as possible so as not to confuse the child.
- Say everything very calmly and keep repeating things calmly.

What works with toddlers?

- Set very clear boundaries.

- Keep as regular a routine as possible.

- Adults working with children should ensure that they are all using the same approach, as children quickly learn how to manipulate adults.

- Ensure the child is clear that the adults are in control and will not give in to any tantrum pressure, however persevering the child is.

- Some children enjoy a picture representation of what is happening that day. A strip of paper could be placed in a specific place with pictures or photographs of what is happening that day. This can be backed with Velcro or Blu-tack. It can be for the whole day or for specific parts of the day such as bedtime. This particular strip of card could show having a bath, getting pyjamas on, story at bedtime, lights out. Sometimes photographs can be used.

- Young children need clear lessons in taking turns and sharing – simple games like rolling a ball to and fro with one child initially and then extending the game to more children in a small group. When playing a game, show and tell the child clearly what the rules are and play with them until you feel they are aware of the rules.

- As soon as young children appear to be aware of rules, leave them when minor squabbles arise and only intervene if the situation becomes difficult.

- Be careful that you do not offer too many choices to a young child. Simple choices like 'We are going to visit Aunty Mary today. Do you want your blue or red socks on?' enable a child to become accustomed to making minor choices. This gives the child the satisfaction of making a choice. Generally a selection of two items should be offered until the child has matured sufficiently to make greater choices.

Good practice in seven simple steps

1. Be consistent.

2. Use praise and rewards.

3. Provide good models.

4. Guide the child.

5. Ignore bad behaviour.

6. Remove from the scene.

7. Apply sanctions.

STEP 1
BE CONSISTENT

Start as you mean to go on and be calm, clear and consistent. Remaining calm and not 'mirroring' the behaviour of a child is a useful tactic when dealing with children who are, for example, having a temper tantrum. Reacting to attention-seeking behaviours in a cool, deliberate manner will have the effect of showing that you are displeased while not giving the child the kind of heightened attention he is seeking. If a child is throwing construction toys for instance, the adult might simply walk up to him, very quietly remind him of the rules and swiftly withdraw the toy as a consequence.

Once the rules in your setting have been established and all staff members know how to deal with certain behaviours, it is vital that everyone responds in the same way. It is very difficult to backtrack once a precedent has been set. For example, if throwing sand is allowed to go unchecked one day, it will encourage children to keep testing the boundaries. As long as everyone knows the rules and how they are to be applied, it will be much easier to be consistent. Children feel secure when they know and understand what the rules are and what is expected of them.

STEP 2
USE PRAISE AND REWARDS

This is the most effective way of reinforcing good behaviour. Always reward the child who tries, to show that she is succeeding and that succeeding is fun. Show the child how pleased you are.

Rewards can be all sorts of things – praise, hugs, smiles, stickers, stars, smiley faces, favourite activities, computer time, reading stories together, choosing time, certificates, etc. How do you decide which to use? Using rewards is very much up to each individual setting. In some settings, it is policy to use only verbal rewards and to acknowledge rather than to praise wanted behaviours. Some children particularly like certain rewards, for example being allowed extra time at a favourite activity, or a 'well done' sticker on their T-shirt. One of the most effective rewards is adult praise or acknowledgement. A simple 'I really liked the way you helped Jack to carry all those toys to the cupboard' can be very effective. Recognizing achievements publicly is a powerful tool for raising self-esteem and motivation. Rewards do not have to be 'big' to have the desired effect. Varying rewards and changing them when they lose impact is important for maintaining motivation; one type of reward does not necessarily fit all children.

Five simple rules for rewards

1. Reward should be immediate: for example, if Jack has in the past been reluctant to tidy up and he is spotted helping to put things away, you could IMMEDIATELY say something like 'Thank you Jack for doing such a good job and making things so tidy.'
2. Reward every time at first and less often when the child finds it easier. If the same reward is given when a child has become better at performing a particular task, the impact is lost. This will have the effect of diminishing motivation on the child's part.
3. Always praise the child when giving rewards.
4. Always say exactly why you're pleased with him. Instead of 'good boy' or 'well done,' say 'I liked the way you waited for Luke to get off the slide before you went down. That was very sensible and grown-up.'
5. Reward children for all different types of good behaviour, so that every child has a chance of being rewarded (see p. 8 for ideas).

Praise

Use the child's name when praising her for doing the right thing. Children who behave badly often hear their names called out (their surnames too sometimes) but well-behaved children can go for days without hearing their name spoken out loud. If you see someone doing something helpful try saying, 'Well done, Kayleigh. That was very kind of you/that looks very neat/etc.' Some children really like to hear their name called for doing the right thing, and this may help to reduce the number of instances of bad behaviour. It also lessens the likelihood that children will be labelled 'naughty Tommy' (to distinguish him from 'reasonably well-behaved Tommy' and 'always well-behaved Tommy').

Positive and specific comments

When praising a child for doing the right thing it is important that she knows exactly what he has done right! Just saying 'Well done, Jamilla' may well mystify some children (especially if they had just done something naughty that you missed). It is far more effective to say, for example, 'Well done, Jamilla, for sitting up so nicely,' or 'Well done, Philip, for lining up so sensibly,' as this will give a much clearer message not only to the target child but also to others standing nearby. Note: children with very low self-esteem sometimes find any kind of praise hard to handle. There can be occasions when adults have commented enthusiastically on a child's painting only to find two minutes later that they have scribbled all over it with black paint. These children need very sensitive handling and may respond better if you praise a couple of children together, for example 'Well done you two for painting such colourful pictures,' or 'Well done all of you who are playing in the sand so sensibly.'

Children can easily miss comments made to them, or questions asked of them, especially if they are engaged in an activity. Saying their name first will alert them: 'Rory . . . Well done, you are getting on really well with your work.' 'Freya . . . Why do you think the baby bear was crying?'

We can praise and reward children for:

- sharing;

- turn-taking;

- tidying up;

- washing paint pots;

- taking a message;

- helping a friend;

- showing kindness;

- asking a good question;

- giving a good answer;

- putting on their own coat;

- remembering to bring something from home;

- noticing something interesting;

- having a good idea;

- being sensible;

- being brave;

- being patient.

STEP 3
PROVIDE GOOD MODELS

Point out to the child someone who is doing well. Praise that person and encourage the child to do the same. Always try to show the child the behaviours you want by commenting when other children are doing the right thing: 'I can see someone sitting very still, listening carefully and looking at me. Well done, Sara.'

When sharing stories, use the characters to share ideas with the child about good and bad behaviour: 'What do you think about Roger not taking his turn to help set the table?' (*It's Your Turn, Roger!* by Susanna Gretz, published by Red Box).

Use the home corner to model good behaviour: 'Thank you for the cup of tea, Ben. You have been so kind to me. Let me do the washing up for you.'

Use puppets to demonstrate good and bad behaviour: 'Susan was very naughty to take the biscuit from Teddy. Teddy is crying now and doesn't want to play with her any more. Let's bring on Kind Kelly to show Susan how to share with friends. Kelly has lots of friends – why do you think everyone likes to play with her?'

STEP 4
GUIDE THE CHILD

For example, when clearing away, show the child step by step and expect him to do it in a similar sequence: 'Well done, Tom, you've sorted out the wax crayons from the pencils. Now let's put the crayons into the red box and the pencils into the tub. Then we can put everything away in the cupboard.'

Help the child to succeed by breaking up tasks into smaller, achievable steps, and praise at each stage. For example, if a child has difficulty sharing toys and pushes others away when they attempt to play, you could at first only expect her to play a simple interactive game such as rolling a ball to another child with adult supervision and then perhaps gradually increase the time and numbers in the group. By introducing different activities and turn-taking in a very small group at first and rewarding each success, you can build upon achievements in a positive manner.

Giving a child take-up time can also help. If you ask a child to do something, particularly if it is something they do not really want to do, it helps if you do not stand over children and watch. Give some take-up time and compliance may well take place without your even having to repeat the instruction. A really big egg timer can also help when you want a particular activity to stop. Advance warning of changes of activity is beneficial in reducing conflict, for example: 'When the sand has gone through I would like you all to be sitting on the carpet/have your coats on.'

When choosing is required, use limited choices such as 'Would you like to play with Lego or the cars?' If too many choices are presented it could encourage lack of focus and 'flitting'. The most difficult times of the day/session for children with behavioural difficulties are the unstructured times, for example free choice and outdoor play. It is during these particular times that the child will need the most direction and support. You could try helping him to plan for himself what he wants to do first – explain the choices and remind him exactly how you expect him to behave: 'We are going outside now, Simon. You could ride on the trike or play on the slide – which one will you choose? If you play on the trike, remember to go round the other children so that you don't bump into them. If you play on the slide, you have to let other children have a go as well, so climb up the steps and slide down when it's your turn. If you stand on the steps all the time, the other children can't have a go.' You may need to repeat the expectation once Simon has chosen his activity and is actually on the equipment.

Plan what you will do with a child who finds it very difficult to move about the setting in an appropriate way. If you are moving from one room to another, support the child by having an adult walking next to her giving prompts or even holding her hand, and modelling the expected behaviour. Praise her if the behaviour is achieved.

STEP 5
IGNORE BAD BEHAVIOUR

Ignore irritating behaviour whenever possible and always try to avoid confrontation. It is often best to ignore the child's behaviour if it is annoying but not too severe, for example a child constantly calling out. Ignoring means not giving any attention and pretending the behaviour is not affecting you at all. Make it clear to the child before the story time or circle time session that he will have a special reward when the story or circle time is finished if he has managed to sit quietly. (Be warned that initially the child's behaviour is likely to become worse as he struggles even harder to get what he wants, especially if he is seeking attention. You have to ignore him every time and make sure he doesn't receive attention from anyone else.)

Tactical ignoring can also avoid drawing everyone's attention to the unwanted behaviour. For instance, if a child is quietly staring into space and not following your instructions, there is no point in saying, 'Stop daydreaming, Lucy.' All that happens then is that everyone near Lucy stops what they are doing to look at her and instead of one child off task you have a whole group. A far more effective strategy is to say, 'Well done, David and Daisy, for tidying up.' Quite often David and Daisy will tidy up even more quickly and happily and with luck, Lucy will stop daydreaming and help too. Similarly, giving out some new crayons or pencils to a group of children actively engaged in a task can be a real incentive to others to settle down and join in.

A lot of children react badly to the word 'No' and have learnt that engaging adults in a lengthy argument will often result in the adult giving in for the sake of a quiet life (the alternative being a major wobbly at the checkout!). By saying 'Yes, when . . .' rather than 'No, because . . .' you can reduce the likelihood of confrontation. For example, if a child wants to play with the Lego but needs to wash the paint off his hands first, try saying, 'Yes, when you've washed your hands, then you can play with the Lego' rather than 'No, because you've got dirty hands.'

Similarly, if a child is in the wrong place doing the wrong thing, for example splashing others by the sink rather than sitting listening to a story, try asking, 'What are you supposed to be doing?' rather than 'Why are you doing that?' 'Why?' questions tend to get in response either a blank stare, one of those irritating shoulder shrugs or an obviously true answer such as 'Because I like splashing water around.' The 'What are you supposed to be doing?' question or 'Can you remember what I asked you to do?' should elicit a more suitable answer.

STEP 6
REMOVE FROM THE SCENE

Removing the child from the situation and giving some 'time out' can prevent escalation of the problem and allow a 'cooling off' time out of sight of the other children. As always, announce 'time out' in a calm voice and reserve it for more serious misdemeanours such as aggression, violence, destructiveness or repeated rudeness.

Time out should be for the minimum possible time – a few minutes are as effective as a longer period. A useful guide is to consider the age of the child. A three-year-old could have a three-minute time-out period. An egg timer could be used to measure this. It should not be a humiliating or scary experience for the child but more a chance to calm down and return to the room to make a fresh start, hopefully with an apology if this is appropriate. Someone should stay with the child and sit nearby, but be careful not to reward with a favourite activity or make things too comfy. Think carefully about what to call the time-out place: the 'peaceful cushion', or the 'quiet place' or the 'calming corner' has more positive connotations than the 'naughty corner'!

STEP 7
APPLY SANCTIONS

Use sanctions only as a last resort. Taking away privileges such as choosing time or a special activity can be powerful in making a point with a child, but may well be counter-productive if she feels embittered about it. With children whose parents frequently use sanctions as a punishment, the impact will be minimal. If you do decide to take this route, make sure the child remembers why this is happening, especially if there has been a time lapse: 'Darren, you won't be having a go on the computer today because you kicked Iqbal and made him cry. I know you like to play on the computer so I hope you will be kind to everyone in nursery tomorrow and then you can have your turn.'

Remember – rewards are much more effective than sanctions so **catch the child being good.**

SOME ADDITIONAL IDEAS

Noise levels

Many children have only two settings on their volume control – VERY LOUD and EVEN LOUDER. Letting off steam and shouting while playing outdoors is very different from doing the same thing indoors with lots of others; some children will need to be shown the difference between an indoor voice and a playground or outdoor voice. It is vital that the adults also demonstrate the difference and refrain from shouting across the room to each other or talking to each other while everyone is supposed to be watching a video for example. A **noisometer** could be positioned on the wall (like a thermometer) with a movable arrow that can be pointed to 'Just Right', 'Getting a Bit Loud' and 'Far Too Noisy'. A traffic light indicator might also be used. One successful strategy is to use a puppet or soft toy which goes into hiding if it gets too noisy and only comes out for a cuddle when things have quietened down again. This seems to work for all ages of children.

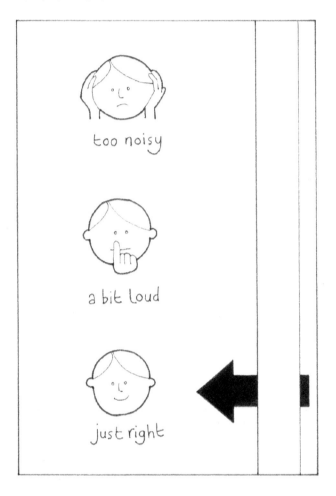

NOISOMETER

too noisy

a bit loud

just right

Chairs

If you are reading a story with the children sitting on the carpet in front of you it is very tempting to tell a fidgety child who is getting on everyone's nerves to go and sit on a chair. Although this might alleviate the situation, there is a fundamental problem with this strategy. By giving the badly behaved child a chair to sit on – which, let's face it, is a lot more comfortable than sitting on a hard floor – we can be seen to be rewarding unwanted behaviour. Try giving the child her own 'sitting spot', a square of carpet or material or a chalk-drawn shape.

Be alert to children becoming uncomfortable – allow them to get up, move about, have a stretch then settle down again. Young children should not be expected to sit still for long periods of time – it's difficult enough for adults!

Playing outdoors

Some children are reasonably well behaved indoors but get completely out of hand in more open spaces, barging into others and spoiling their games. It may be worth considering some form of 'passport' which they give to the outside supervisor, who puts a smiley face on the passport if they have a good playtime. Five smiley faces result in a special certificate, star or choice of favourite activity. Teaching children how to play simple games can help with problems like this (Oranges and Lemons, Old Macdonald, What's the Time Mr Wolf?) and getting them to run around (all the same way) for a few minutes helps to burn off excess energy.

Rules

If your setting has some clearly displayed and easily understood rules you can save a lot of unnecessary dialogue by simply repeating the rule. If a child is swearing or shouting, rather than admonishing him you can say: 'We speak kindly,' or 'We play carefully and safely.'

In brief

- Make sure rules are known and understood by the children, parents and all staff – revisit them often.

- Use a home-school liaison book for positive behaviours/achievements to share with parents/carers and in the setting.

- Use a high degree of structure for children with behaviour problems.

- Give responsibility to children with behavioural difficulties, for example by appointing them as the helper at snack time.

- Use favourite activities as rewards.

- Use visual aids wherever possible, e.g. if giving instructions about washing hands, show a picture of the children using the wash area.

- Use a personal carpet square or 'spot' for children who have problems sitting still for a story.

- Use a variety of rewards and change them when they lose impact.

- Use extension activities – keep a box of resources ready and add to it over time.

- Make sure children know what you mean if you have to tell them off. 'Stop that' is not enough – 'Stop throwing sand' will send the message to all the children.

- Following a request, say 'thank you'; this implies that the request will be carried out.

Quick tips for establishing good relationships

- Be positive and generous with praise.

- Be careful how you talk to people. It is much better to say 'You will find it easier if . . .' rather than 'Don't do it like that.' Remember, an unkind word lingers much longer than a kind one.

- Label the act NOT the child, e.g. 'Pushing Fred was a dangerous thing to do,' rather than 'YOU are a bully.' Negative labels stick.

- Build in success. Make sure that programmes of work enable all children to succeed in some way.

- Think back. Remember your own schooldays? Teachers are the creators of memories – make sure that your setting is a happy one. Do not be afraid to have some fun.

- Smile. Non-verbal messages are important to children. A pat on the back, a smile, a nod gives as much encouragement as words.

- Children often have the answer. After an incident, ask the child, 'Why might I be angry now?' Encourage children to analyse their own behaviour and begin to take responsibility for it.

Quick tips for raising self-esteem

- Celebrate children's differences and unique personalities – don't expect every child to behave/respond in the same way.

- Find something to praise in every child, every day.

- Look at every child – establish eye contact as often as possible.

- Make time to listen to children as well as talk to them.

- Take their feelings seriously by noticing and acknowledging feelings whether good or bad.

Things to say
'I expect you are feeling . . . now.'
'That must be upsetting . . . do you want to tell me about it?'
'You seem . . .'
'You look . . .'

Autistic Spectrum Disorder and speech and language difficulties, delay and disorders

Autistic Spectrum Disorder

Some suggestions for supporting children in early years settings with ASD

Speech and language difficulties, delay and disorders

Vocabulary used to describe speech and language issues

Some suggestions for supporting children in early years settings with speech and language difficulties

Case study: Oral dyspraxia

Autistic Spectrum Disorder (ASD) and speech and language difficulties have been presented together here in order to highlight the potential complexities of identification. It can be difficult, especially in the pre-verbal child, to differentiate between behaviours that look similar but that may have a very different cause. It is not unusual for children with difficulties like ASD and severe speech and language disorders to have complex, overlapping conditions (comorbidity). Speech and language disorder and delay are the most commonly identified issues in the pre-school phase, but in very young children, it is important to remember that behaviours described here can be ascribed to children developing entirely within the typical range.

It should be stressed that this book is not a tool for diagnosis but rather a guide for addressing behaviours that cause concern. Observations should be carried out over a period of time so that any concerns around development can contribute to a meaningful gathering of evidence. It is likely that the core difficulty in the development of a child will emerge over time. It may then be easier to differentiate between any potential difficulty. It is even more important to be thorough in any observation and assessment carried out in the case of pre-verbal children. These issues need to be taken into consideration for any future interventions to be successful. Professional advice and support should always be sought, and early intervention often has the best outcome. Some case studies in Section 3 can be linked to areas discussed in the following section.

Autistic Spectrum Disorder

Here we will concentrate on the most often observed traits of autism in young children. Diagnosis of Autistic Spectrum Disorder (ASD) in children is usually made by a paediatrician with the support of a speech and language therapist and an educational psychologist along with practitioners such as teachers and early years specialists in some cases.

ASD is defined by a difficulty with speech and language, social interaction and communication, and a lack of imagination. There are a range of descriptions used to describe ASD. Pathological Demand Avoidance, Pervasive Developmental Disorder, Kanners Autism, Classic Autism and Asperger's Syndrome are some that are commonly heard. We will use the term, Autistic Spectrum Disorder (ASD) since this is the most commonly used term when a diagnosis is made.

It is worth stating that all children are unique and not every child on the autistic spectrum exhibits the same behaviours although there are some traits that are usually common to a large number of individuals. Autistic children are as unique and different as every other child. Indeed, some people on the autistic spectrum often describe themselves as having specific abilities that have had a positive effect upon their development and their lives. The new buzzword, 'neuro diversity', is being seen on more applications for employment and is a welcome addition to the vocabulary. The autistic spectrum is a vast one. At the severe end are children with little or no language and severe learning difficulties, while at the other are children who can be highly articulate and intelligent. These individuals are able to manage their condition effectively and lead happy, fulfilled lives. Indeed, some believe that the line between a diagnosable condition at the high-functioning end of the spectrum and a personality trait can be vague. The identification of Autistic Spectrum Disorder in settings is becoming more common since practitioners receive more training and thus awareness is raised. Autism is a lifelong condition.

Speech and language

If we take speech and language associated with autism in the first instance we may observe many variations. There may be a complete lack of speech sounds, there may be high-pitched noises that appear to have little significance to the observer, there may be other noises or vocalizations that appear random in nature. There may be a few single words or short phrases that are used to highlight personal need. In the case of children with some language, there may be an odd quality to speech, for example, a sing-song delivery, a flat, monotone delivery. There could be phrases uttered out of context, there may be odd pitch, rhythm, lack of intonation to speech. Repetitive phrases or sentences can sometimes be observed or random, learned phrases that could appear out of context. For children with higher levels of language one can often observe highly specialized language, especially if a child has obsessional interests, and these children will often exhibit good levels of language in relation to their interests but struggle with spontaneous conversation and answers to simple questions. Questions may be ignored, or they may be answered with an out of context response. Language may be idiosyncratic, there may be a wide vocabulary especially relating to topics of interest. These children are often very good at responding to factual questions or concrete information but can struggle to expand upon this initial communication. When asked indirect questions about their interests a child like this may ignore the communication or return to a more comfortable, familiar pattern of communicating. For example, a child who is asked 'what is that' may well answer correctly but when asked 'what do we do with it', may struggle. Some children understand that an answer is required and provide one that is confusing to the questioner. Repeating phrases or questions (echolalia) or sentences learned by heart from a favourite film or song is not unusual. For higher functioning children, open-ended communications can be difficult. For example, when asked 'what could happen . . . ' or 'what do you think might happen . . ..' children can struggle to provide an appropriate response because such questions and interactions don't have factual right or wrong answers.

Understanding language

For children on the autistic spectrum understanding language may be difficult. For example, it may be easy for children to carry out a simple instruction correctly, that is, an instruction containing a single element. When an instruction contains more than one element (complex instruction) children will often ignore the instruction or carry out the last heard element. For example, 'get shoes' may be easier to understand than 'get your blue shoes from upstairs and put them in the car'. Ambiguous language can also lead to misunderstanding. Language may be taken literally; for example, 'pull your socks up' may often lead to a child doing just that but missing out on the intended point being made. A teacher using the phrase 'no more talking' may lead to a child doing exactly that with unforeseen consequences. Higher functioning children with ASD may have difficulties understanding figurative language, sarcasm, inference, idioms, metaphors and so on.

Social interaction

Children with autism often exhibit the following: a lack of eye contact, fleeting eye contact, prolonged eye contact, a preference for being alone, playing alone with a restricted range of toys, a dislike of noisy environments or highly stimulating environments for example, supermarkets. Children avoid social contact in any form, particularly those including large groups, parties or social gatherings. They may exhibit inappropriate social interactions; for example, overly affectionate behaviour that is indiscriminate, a lack of awareness of  people's names, ignoring of peers and adults, especially those adults who do not meet an individual's needs. There may be overly attached behaviour toward one particular child. Distress may be a feature of some children's behaviour especially when changes to routines occur. Children may struggle to make and to maintain relationships, to engage in conversation and information sharing and to understand facial expressions and body language.

Asperger's Syndrome

Children with a diagnosis of Asperger's Syndrome may be referred to as having 'high-functioning autism'. These children often have high levels of language and some favoured methods of interaction. They may present with some eye contact – this can be fleeting or prolonged. Children at this end of the spectrum are often seen as being able to cope in a mainstream environment but still struggle with communicating, social interaction, forming relationships and reaching their potential while coping with difficult issues around their autism. Most children with Asperger's Syndrome require a tailored, individualized plan of intervention in educational settings in order to manage and meet their needs. Children often present with the following: varied levels of eye contact, withdrawing and wanting to be alone, a lack of empathy, a social unawareness, unwillingness to join in with groups or parties, the use of jargon or learned phrases, taking language literally, rambling off topic, out of context communication, the tone and voice levels may be neutral or high pitched or delivered in a monotone, not waiting for responses to questions, interrupting and blurting out responses. Social interactions may well be seen as inappropriate or clumsy.

Behaviours associated with ASD

Although no two autistic children are the same there are some behaviours that are routinely observed. This may include a liking for predictability and routine, a liking for order (for example, lining up toys or objects and not actually playing with them as intended), a lack of role play or imaginative play, repetitive actions, a dislike of noisy environments and avoidance of large groups. There may be a liking for the way light filters through windows or other objects. There may be a liking for spinning objects, flapping objects or flapping hands. Some children routinely put their hands over their ears, ignoring peers and/or adults. There may be restricted use of language (e.g. used to meet personal needs only), the continued use of single words, obsessional behaviours, sensory difficulties.

Sensory issues relating to children with ASD

Some children have a liking for a restricted range of textures in clothing; for example, some dislike clothing labels or certain fibres, such as wool that they feel is rough, or anything causing irritation. Some children demand an extremely restricted range of food or will only eat one type of food; for example they will only eat foods that are the same colour, that do not touch on their plates, that have similar consistency. Some children exhibit an intolerance or aversion to certain objects, textures, lighting and noises. Some children refuse to engage in activities that are messy; for example, painting, gluing, baking, etc. It is not unusual to observe children in exciting, noisy, busy nurseries sitting by themselves with their hands over their ears in an attempt to reduce the sensory stimulation in their environment.

The lack of imagination associated with ASD

At first glance, this appears to be a rather unimportant 'difficulty' associated with ASD when one considers the enormous impact that speech, language and social interaction can have. However, when it is more closely considered, this area of development can have a significant impact upon the individual. For example, a lack of role play may be observed in young children. Solitary play or a lack of cooperative play is also a feature. Role and imaginative play has an important impact upon the development of very young children and repetitive play is often a feature observed in children with ASD. Children with a lack of imagination have difficulty in understanding that others can have a different opinion to themselves or indeed that there is any other opinion apart from that held by the child themselves. That is to say, the opinion held by a child with ASD is seen as a fact by the individual. Theory of mind (the ability to realise that others have differing opinions) is a real challenge to lots of children (and adults) with ASD. The current definition of theory of mind is 'the ability to ascribe mental states to other persons and how we use this to predict the actions of those persons. It is the ability to attribute the beliefs, intents and knowledge that are different to one's own'. This can often result in difficulties with empathy, the notion that others may be pretending, a difficulty understanding that there can be several different outcomes to questions and that there can sometimes be no right or wrong conclusion. The ability to have empathy is an issue for lots of children and can lead to a lack of interest in peers, a lack of compassion when other children are hurt, a lack of ability to share and to take turns, and an inflexibility of thought. The lack of ability to use the imagination can have catastrophic effects in later life since if language is taken literally and there is little empathy for others, then a very gullible, impressionable youngster may be led into activities that are inappropriate.

The impact of a diagnosis of ASD

For the parents of a child with ASD, a diagnosis can be viewed in very different ways. Most parents will tell you that they had always known that there were problems or differences. Some parents are relieved to get a diagnosis since they struggled to make sense of their child's behaviour and a diagnosis helps to come to terms with this. Some parents are worried by a diagnosis and have had little knowledge or experience of ASD. Some parents are relieved to hear that whatever their child's difficulties, that they, as parents, have not caused them and they are not 'at fault'.

For settings and practitioners, a diagnosis can help with the management of children with ASD. Care should be taken to address the needs of the individual so that programmes of intervention are personalized since all children with ASD are different. Children with ASD can demonstrate comorbidity, that is a complex 'overlapping' of additional conditions. It should be stressed that although practitioners in early years settings are often the first to raise concerns about children's development, they should always avoid attempts to 'diagnose'. Their job is to discuss any concerns with parents and professionals and to restrict themselves to what has been observed. Parents' wishes for any further interventions should always be paramount. Some parents opt for special education when mainstream school is not seen as appropriate. Depending upon the protocol in Local Education Areas, statutory assessment may be an option, especially when a diagnosis is a prerequisite for access to a special school. Statutory assessment or the Education and Health Care Plan is discussed briefly in Section 8. It should be stressed that descriptions of behaviours and developmental issues discussed earlier in this chapter can also be attributed to typically developing children. The main difference is that these behaviours are fleeting for the typically developing child and give way to 'next step' milestones. Any significant, ongoing developmental issue is likely to have an impact upon the progress of young children and upon their ability to access the Early Years Curriculum. Professional support should always be sought with the agreement of parents.

Advantages for children with ASD and Asperger's Syndrome

Some children and adults with a diagnosis of ASD will often cite several positive advantages to being on the spectrum, such as liking for detail and order, an ability to focus for prolonged periods on special interests, the ability to use special areas of interest to engage in projects, a highly developed ability to take in information that is of interest. The autistic savant is a rare condition. True savants have extraordinary abilities (usually in narrow fields) and can demonstrate prodigious  abilities that are incongruous when compared to their overall difficulties. While Savant Syndrome is rare, it is not uncommon for children with ASD to have a great deal of knowledge about their special interests or obsessions.

Some suggestions for supporting children in early years settings with ASD

Since all children demonstrate a unique set of behaviours and difficulties and develop at different rates, any support plan should leave room for adaptations to accommodate progress. Intervention in the early years is vital to provide a solid foundation for future education. Children who are used to good levels of support that are successful, will be more confident in managing their condition later on in their school careers. Managing suggestions that are good for children with ASD tend to be useful for all children in the early years. Children with additional needs benefit from added structure to learning, and to the timetable including unstructured times of the day, such as playtimes and times for managing personal needs. Strategies like this can help children to predict what may happen and to feel more secure.

The environment

Section 4 of this book contains some general managing strategies with regard to the learning environment. The following may provide some more specific strategies for the child with ASD:

- Label everything.
- Use visual clues for names on clothes pegs.
- Use visual aids to accompany verbal instructions.
- Implement a pictorial timetable of the session and discuss with the group using vocabulary like 'now', 'next', 'before', 'after'.

- Implement visual cards to use with the pictorial timetable that include changes to routines.
- Provide role models.
- Provide sequential pictures for dressing, washing, etc. These may be stuck to the mirror over hand basins or whereever required.

Pictorial timetables

The use of the pictorial timetable is a major resource and aid for children with ASD. This can be used at home or at nursery/school and can be extended to meet the ongoing needs of the individual.

At first, the pictures on the timetable should indicate 'chunks' of the session. For example if there is a natural pause in the session (snack times, group time, etc.), the timetable should concentrate upon the first few events. This will help children to sequence and to predict what will happen without overloading them. So, the first picture/s might indicate being greeted in the nursery and where to hang your coat. The next picture might indicate play and the following one might indicate group time. A box containing pictures of events in the nursery should be nearby and the child with ASD should be encouraged to help to sort pictures into the predicted events of the session and to include these onto the pictorial timetable. The support worker should use the vocabulary 'first', 'next', 'after'. The timetable should always include a picture of parents collecting their children at the end of the session since children with ASD often have difficulty with the concept of time passing, for example that the session will actually have an ending. Similarly, when a change to events occurs, a picture should be used to discuss this and also when it will happen. If an outing is planned, it should be made clear (via the timetable) that the group will be returning to nursery. When children are comfortable with the use of a pictorial timetable (and this may take several months), the time covered by the timetable can be extended gradually. Children with ASD may require individual timetables to be drawn up and they may require several reminders about what is happening with regard to events. Pictorial timetables work best when used regularly and when all staff are consistent about their use.

If the same strategy is used at home, the usefulness of the pictorial timetable is extended. Parents with children who are distressed by visits to the supermarket for instance, say that since implementing a visual method of helping children to predict events has made a difference. Sequential pictures of daily events like washing hands, cleaning teeth and getting dressed can be helpful for developing independence.

Managing strategies for encouraging language

For children with very limited language:

- Use visual aids for every communication combined with role modelling.
- Use simple instructions (instructions containing one element) and stick to key words for example, 'get coat'. These instructions should be accompanied by guiding every time at first.
- Use praise every time.

- Use signing to accompany speech.
- Stick to key words for making personal needs known, e.g. 'more', 'again', 'drink', 'biscuit', etc.
- Implement visual aids specifically designed to help children make needs known.
- Avoid negatives for example, instead of saying 'no' or 'don't do that . . . ' say 'do this . . . ' or 'thanks for doing . . .'
- Implement a 'first this and then' card to help with sequencing events or following adult-led activities.
- Use choice making whenever possible. For example, 'want the red car or blue car' and accompany with the real objects/toys.

For children with some language:

- Extend language skills by modelling speech, especially when describing actions. This works best when playing alongside.
- Identify objects and describe what they are used for.
- Use pictures to sequence events and describe these.
- Use more complex instructions and gradually increase these.
- Use very clear, unambiguous language.
- Praise frequently.

Strategies for supporting social development

- Use pictures/photos of people depicting a range of emotions and help children to identify these using a single word.
- Use social stories and comic strips to describe what is happening.
- Implement a social skills programme to help interaction.
- Teach typical interactions directly. For example, upon meeting new people we say 'hello, how are you' 'my name is . . . '. If someone asks if you would like a biscuit or crackers, we say 'crackers please', etc. Children with ASD may require a role model for most interactions at first.
- Help children to use some eye contact by asking them to look at your glasses/ hair if appropriate. Some children find this very difficult and they should never be made to do this if it is felt that they are distressed.
- Use tasks that include shared attention, turn taking and group activities. Group sizes should be increased gradually.

Speech and language difficulties, delay and disorders

The subject of speech and language development is a vast and serious subject and we do not intend to replicate the many excellent text books available on the market. In this section we will attempt to clarify the difference between delay and disorder for the early years practitioner and outline some common speech and language difficulties observed in children. We will suggest some strategies that may help to manage these.

Speech is about the sounds that are made. This is a problem when the sounds made are not understood by others.

Language is often seen as a measure of intelligence and delays in language development are more serious than a specific delay with the production of speech sounds. A language delay is language development in the right sequence but at a slower rate. Delayed speech and language is the most common developmental problem in young children.

Speech and Language Disorder describes speech and language development that is not within the normal range or presents as atypical.

There are many things that can affect the development of speech and language: hearing loss, generalized developmental delay, prematurity, auditory processing difficulties, neurological problems, brain injury, cerebral palsy, autism, neglect. Hearing should be checked in the first instance since this is one of the most common things that affects speech and language development. The advice and support of a speech and language therapist should always be sought if concerns are raised.

If a child presents with a generalized or global developmental delay, we would expect language development to be commensurate with this.

Vocabulary used to describe speech and language issues

Speech – refers to the sounds used in oral communication – how we say it.

Language – refers to the words and sentences – what we say.

Phonology – refers to the speech sounds system.

Phonology processes – exist to make it easier to learn to speak; for example, 'nana' is easier to say than 'banana'.

Phoneme – individual speech sounds.

Phonological delay – describes a child displaying speech patterns typical of a younger child.

Phonological disorder – implies there is a problem of some sort, either due to excessive delay or speech patterns unlike those of a typically developing child.

Articulation – the control of tongue, lips, teeth and palate (articulators) to produce speech sounds.

Articulation disorder – occurs where there is a difficulty in making sounds. This may be due to a structural abnormality such as cleft lip and palate.

Dyspraxia – is a difficulty carrying out volitional movements required for speech in the absence of abnormalities of speech musculature.

> **Dysarthria** – describes motor speech disorder which stems from neuro-logical damage; for example, cerebral palsy.
>
> **Intelligibility** – how easy it is to understand someone's speech.
>
> **Consonant clusters** – two or more consonants together for example, st ar, str aw, mi st.
>
> **Segmentation** – breaking words into syllables, for example, el e phant – breaking words into phonemes (sounds) c a t.
>
> Note: Thank you to Medway Speech and Language Therapy Department for providing information for settings in Medway, including information on the vocabulary above.

The speech and language therapist can provide support for children demonstrating speech, language and communication problems. Some important early skills for language development are eye contact, attention and listening skills, turn taking, copying, play, babble and gesture.

It is important to say that if a child presents with a significant speech problem, even if this includes speech that is completely unintelligible, this is not always a reflection of the child's overall abilities or of their intelligence. Specific speech difficulties, for example, oral dyspraxia (a motor coordination problem that can make speech extremely difficult to understand), would be characterized as a *specific learning difficulty* (SpLD) for educational purposes. It is not uncommon for these children to be assessed as progressing within the typical range across the curriculum with the exception of specifically associated areas (speaking and listening). Some terms used to describe speech problems can be confusing; for example, verbal and oral dyspraxia. Verbal dyspraxia refers to a difficulty making and coordinating the precise movements required for the production of clear speech sounds. Oral dyspraxia refers to a difficulty making and coordinating the movements of the vocal tract (larynx, lips, tongue and palate). For example, a child demonstrating oral dyspraxia may present with excessive drooling and may have difficulty with licking, sucking, blowing and any tongue or lip movement. This is an oro motor coordination difficulty. A referral to a speech and language therapist would be advisable in such circumstances. There are some rare disorders such as mutism or selective mutism. This is a condition where a child only speaks in very specific circumstances. For example, the child may only speak when at home and not in nursery. This is not seen as a speech and language disorder but rather an anxiety issue since speaking is not the problem. If the problem persists and is impacting upon the child's progress with education and social communication and interaction, help and advice should be sought from a specialist. In the first instance it will be helpful if a referral to a speech and language therapist can be made. The therapist will be able to make a diagnosis and is likely to be able to make further referrals for interventions. It is important to identify the problem early since mutism can affect children later on in their school careers.

Some suggestions for supporting children in early years settings with speech and language difficulties

Encouraging attention and listening skills

Play musical games – guess the sound or instrument, copying a sequence or the rhythm of sounds, sound lotto, Simon Says, etc. Encourage listening by positioning yourself at the child's level, use simple language to describe what you are doing, make use of intonation, facial expressions and gesture, ensure there are not too many distractions and use fewer toys when playing listening games.

Symbolic play skills

Use large dolls or teddies, feed, dress and wash them, make pretend beds, take them for a walk in a toy pram, act out nursery routines, play hospitals, have pretend tea parties, picnics, etc. Use miniature toy play, match the toy, match items and objects in dolls house, match pictures, make a house from boxes, match animal toys to each other and then to pictures, sort animals into families, use construction toys like Lego to make cars, houses, towers, etc.

Turn taking

At first, use simple language and say 'my turn', 'Sophie's turn' when engaged in play. Wait for full attention before commencing play. Later, children can be encouraged to take turns by playing with one other child on a see saw or simple board game. Gradually increase the size of groups so that children get used to waiting for their turn. Make sure there are not too many distractions nearby. Some children may require demonstrations of activities initially so that they understand what is expected.

Nursery by Isabella

CASE STUDY

Oral dyspraxia

Cameron (four years old) is a bright and enthusiastic member of his nursery. He is popular with peers and adults and engages in all activities with great curiosity and energy. Cameron's progress across the Early Years Curriculum is recorded as average to above average with the exception of speaking. Cameron attempts speech and, although this is mostly unintelligible, he continues to attempt this form of communication. Cameron makes his needs known to adults by the use of gesture and some signing. Cameron often dribbles excessively. Although Cameron is not able to make himself understood by speaking to peers, his excellent social skills have made up for this and he is able to engage socially with them albeit with added effort on his part.

Strategies:

- Teach Cameron to sign but encourage his attempts to speak alongside this.
- Never correct speech but rather, model correct speech.
- Implement a programme of exercises to promote oro motor control, e.g. blowing bubbles in water using a range of different size straws, blowing ping pong balls using straws, play blow football, play the harmonica and blow whistles, blow up balloons, practise biting, crunching and chewing, practise tongue exercises.
- Be aware that children like Cameron use a great deal of energy communicating and he may require 'time out' occasionally in order to 'recharge'.
- It is essential that a referral to a speech and language therapist is made with parental consent in order to meet Cameron's needs. He is likely to require ongoing therapy and the advice of a speech and language therapist in order to make progress with this specific difficulty. Programmes can be carried out at home and at the nursery.

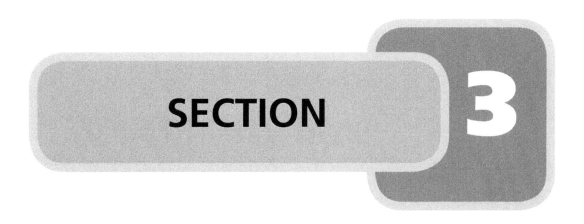

SECTION 3

Real children in real settings

Behaviours that cause concern
and strategies for coping

Playground setting by Eden

CASE STUDY 1

Quiet, withdrawn behaviour

William spends much of his time at pre-school in the book area on his own. He watches the other children but will not respond when they try to talk to him. He hides his face and looks the other way when children try to talk and play with him. Most children now leave him on his own.

Possible reasons for this behaviour:

- Shyness may be a part of William's personality.
- Does William get attention at home for this behaviour?
- William has difficulty with understanding language.
- William has difficulty with social skills; he may not have had a lot of social contact before joining pre-school and needs time to adjust to a busy environment.
- Withdrawn behaviour may indicate some more serious underlying problems at home if it persists over several weeks in spite of appropriate responses by staff.

Strategies:

- Avoid pressurizing him – he may need time to settle and just watch for a while, joining in when he is ready.
- Talk with parents/carers and find out how William behaves at home. A home visit can often tell you a great deal.
- Check that his hearing is not impaired.
- Encourage William to play with one child initially, alongside each other with Lego (or similar). Gradually introduce some cooperative element such as building a fort together.
- Monitor William's behaviour when on his own or when encouraged by an adult, to find out what he enjoys doing.
- Praise him whenever he is with other children.
- Introduce a 'special friend' for the day who will help William to join in with activities.
- (Add your own ideas here).

CASE STUDY 2

Attention-seeking behaviour

As soon as Tara comes into pre-school she seeks an adult and will not leave her mother until she is holding the hand of another adult. She will only play or do activities when an adult is near her, and constantly looks out for adults. Whenever she does a puzzle she looks at the adult before she puts the pieces in the slots. When the adult moves away she will just sit and do nothing or watch for the adult coming back.

Possible reasons for this behaviour:

- Coming into a new environment and feeling insecure is the primary reason for this sort of behaviour. It is important to be patient and allow enough time for children to feel at home with new surroundings and unfamiliar people.
- Adults at home have done most things for her and not encouraged independence.
- She is the youngest in the family, where she is treated as 'the baby', and wants to maintain this level of attention.
- Receptive language difficulties – not understanding what adults are saying and therefore unsure about what she should be doing.

Strategies:

- Find out about the family situation and try to work out a simple plan to encourage independence at home. For example, the first emphasis could be on Tara attempting to do a puzzle or play with a toy by herself. She should be praised every time an adult notices her trying to do this on her own.
- Implement an intensive praise and reinforcement schedule so that Tara begins to recognize all the good things she is doing. Initially it will be important to praise Tara for every single thing she attempts and draw her attention to the way she is progressing. In this way she will gain self-confidence.
- Design a specific programme for Tara coming into the pre-school. When she is greeted by an adult worker she could then be introduced to another child and the two children could be

encouraged to play with something they enjoy or to share a story together.

- Work out a simple recording system so that Tara and her parents/carers become aware of how she is progressing. A simple star or sticker chart will serve as a record of how many times Tara has tried to do things on her own – but be aware that stickers do not work as a reward for all children.

CASE STUDY 3

Screaming

Most of the time, Kieran really enjoys pre-school. He is a lively boy with lots of friends and loves the big equipment such as the slides and scooters. He is very happy playing with things he enjoys. The problem starts when he is asked to do some table-top activities. He starts to scream really loudly so that many children stop what they are doing. This can go on for about 15 minutes.

Possible reasons for this behaviour:

- This is learnt behaviour from home – if he screams for long enough he will get what he wants.
- He is attention-seeking and knows that if he screams people will watch him.
- He has difficulty with some table-top activities and does not like seeing other children doing things better than him. He is afraid of failure. He has difficulties with following instructions.

Strategies:

- Remove any audience if possible and ensure the other children are engaged in their own activities. If you have an area or another room available, move the other children away, leaving one adult to watch over Kieran.
- Encourage Kieran to sit in a quiet area until he is ready to join in. This needs to be explained to him before any screaming sessions start so that he is aware that he can have some time to think about what he is doing.
- Use a visual timetable so that Kieran can choose his own activities for the session but ensure that he understands that he must include at least one table-top activity. In this way he is becoming involved in making his own choices but with the understanding that it includes a range of activities.
- Use a visual timetable on which the order of events is clearly displayed. Kieran can then finish each section before moving on to the next section.
- Reward him on any occasion that he does cooperate with table-top activities.

CASE STUDY 4

Kicking

Dominic enjoys the big toys at pre-school. He likes the slide and playing chasing games with two other boys. If he is asked to come along to a table-top activity and he does not want to, he will kick out at the pre-school worker and refuse to go. If he wants to play with a particular toy and other children will not let him, he will kick those children and also bite them. He has been known to bite adults.

Possible reasons for this behaviour:

- Dominic has learnt that he gets to do things he wants to when he kicks and bites.
- Dominic has had no models of sharing and insufficient positive experience of sharing.
- He does not consider the feelings of others and finds it difficult to respond to meaningful social situations.

Strategies:

- Dominic will need praise whenever he plays well with other children and responds to adult requests. ('Well done, Dominic, I like the way you waited for Sean to get off the trike – isn't he kind to let you have a go.')
- There will need to be clear rules in place at pre-school so that Dominic is fully aware of expectations of his behaviour. These rules will need to include how to relate to other children when they are playing with toys and how to ask them politely if he wants to play with a toy they have. Some stories and (puppet) role-play may prove useful.
- Dominic will need to learn that kicking and biting is unacceptable behaviour, and clear consequences should be in place for when he does bite or kick. It will be important that he does not receive additional adult attention for his biting or kicking.
- Dominic may benefit from specific sessions to teach social skills such as turn-taking and sharing equipment. These could be carried out in small groups focusing on a specific theme, such as when a child wants to play with a toy that someone else has. Role-play would be helpful.
- Keep pointing out children who are playing nicely and who are able to share toys so that Dominic becomes fully aware of what is expected of him.

CASE STUDY 5

Short attention

Rehanah cannot sit still and listen to a story at story time. She constantly shuffles about on her hands and knees, disturbing the children around her. She does not seem to notice that other children are trying to listen to the story. She constantly shouts out and interrupts the story and tries to talk about irrelevant things.

Possible reasons for this behaviour:

- Rehanah has little experience of listening to stories and group situations.
- She has hearing difficulties.
- She is attention-seeking.
- Receptive language problems may hinder the understanding of language. Rehanah may not understand every word in a sentence when being spoken to; she may only understand one or two key words, making stories very difficult to follow.
- Rehanah may have difficulty with the social rules of behaviour, e.g. not butting in when others are talking.
- This very immature behaviour could be a reflection of her general cognitive abilities.

Strategies:

- Give her a special place to sit, such as on a cushion, and let her hold a special toy so that 'Teddy' can listen to the story too. Initially, expect Rehanah to sit for a short length of time such as three minutes with an adult nearby. Gradually the time can be extended and the adult can move farther away. If she manages to sit still for the required time, give her a reward.
- Suggest to her parents/carers that they arrange for an eye test and/ or hearing test via the GP. If the behaviour continues despite clear expectations and a carefully structured behaviour plan, it may be helpful for her to sit near an adult reading the story so that she can see the pictures more clearly or be more involved in the process by helping to turn the pages over. In this way she will be given special responsibility and can be praised.
- Give praise whenever Rehanah is sitting still and looks as if she is listening, so that she receives attention whenever she is being

'good'. She may need to be shown very clearly what 'being good' is. When possible, ignore her shuffling.

- Point out children who are sitting nicely and listening so that Rehanah is clear about expectations. It can be helpful to remind children before the story of the way to listen: 'Bottoms on the floor, lips together, eyes looking at me' – with appropriate gestures. Try asking them a specific question at the beginning. In this way they are listening out for something specific in the story-telling.

- Let Rehanah become accustomed to listening to stories by sitting in a small group or one-to-one with an adult so that she gets used to listening to the whole story. Start with very short stories. Stories recorded on tape and heard through headphones can be useful.

- Praise her whenever you see her sitting still.

- Have a clear system in place for whenever Rehanah is causing disruption such as sitting her on her own away from the group with a book.

- Use a real photograph (with parents' permission) of Rehanah sitting still to act as a prompt: 'Look, Rehanah, here you are sitting very still. I hope you will be sitting like this while I read the story today.'

- Monitor her rate of learning. If she has difficulty in naming colours, learning simple rhymes, constructing simple phrases, the inattentive behaviour may be part of a general learning difficulty.

CASE STUDY 6

Temper tantrums

Danny finds change very difficult to handle and can suddenly explode if asked to stop what he is doing. In the past few days this has become of serious concern and he has kicked adults and children when asked to stop throwing sand around the room.

Possible reasons for this behaviour:

- A change of circumstances at home is making him unsettled.
- He is young – lack of maturity.
- Circumstances have changed at pre-school.
- Is there a medical reason – is he in pain/not feeling well?
- He may be showing signs of ASD.

Strategies:

- Give warnings about changes to routine or activity at 5–10 minute intervals so Danny begins to start thinking about doing something different.
- Explain beforehand about expected behaviour.
- Make consequences very clear.
- Use a visual timetable and make it personal with prompts if needed.
- Ask Danny directly why he is behaving as he is – what is bothering him?
- Reassure him.

CASE STUDY 7

Oppositional behaviour

Rajinder frequently refuses point blank to comply with the most reasonable of requests, e.g. 'Come and join us in the story corner.' She sits on the floor with her head down and refuses to make eye contact. She will keep this up for an hour or more. If attempts are made to move her she will cling to the leg of a table.

Possible reasons for this behaviour:

- She has social communication problems.
- There are serious problems within the family.
- She has difficulties in understanding the social organization of the pre-school, e.g. there may be a lack of experience of social groups. Rajinder may never have had contact with large groups of children and adults who are not part of her family.
- There could be cultural differences that Rajinder finds unfamiliar.
- There may be undetected speech and language problems associated with processing language and understanding what is being said.

Strategies:

- Ask parents/carers if they know why she is behaving like this.
- Arrange for speech and language assessment.
- Suggest to parents/carers that they arrange a hearing assessment via their GP.
- Introduce a buddy system so that another child steers her in the right direction.
- Find out what she enjoys doing at home, and bring into pre-school.
- Use a visual timetable so she becomes aware of the structure of the day.
- Where possible, give her a choice, e.g. 'Rajinder, would you like to sit next to me in the story corner, or next to Simon?' 'Would you like to join us in the story corner, or look at a book by yourself?'
- Give a warning when activities are going to stop, e.g. 'In two minutes' time when you hear the rain stick, we are going to tidy up.'

CASE STUDY 8

Selective mutism

Andy appears to understand what is being said to him and will join in most activities. He will not, however, speak to anyone, adult or child, in the pre-school setting. His mother reports that he chats away merrily at home.

Possible reasons for this behaviour:

- Andy uses this as a controlling mechanism.
- Andy fears failure – it could be safer not to talk.
- He may be intimidated by some/all children in the setting.

Strategies:

- Never try to 'force' Andy to speak or draw attention to his unwillingness to speak.
- Suggest someone from home comes to the pre-school to talk to Andy so that he can speak with someone familiar while in the setting.
- Ensure there are some non-verbal systems in place (e.g. PECS, see 'Appendix 3: Useful addresses').
- Be prepared to be patient over a long period.
- Use puppets as a method of communicating.
- After a period of time, if things do not improve, Andy may need some professional help.

CASE STUDY 9

Sharing

Peter will not share anything; he snatches toys out of the hands of other children and has been known to take small objects home (pieces of Lego, etc.) hidden in his pockets.

Possible reasons for this behaviour:

- It may be his age – immaturity.
- Peter possibly has low self-esteem.
- There are deprived circumstances in the home.
- He feels insecure.
- He is seeking attention.

Strategies:

- Explain clearly where items and equipment should be put after use.
- Ask Peter why he likes to take things home. Is there a toy library he could use? Are there any story sacks he could take home?
- Make a 'borrowing bag' for Peter – allow him to borrow books and toys overnight but insist that he brings them back the next day. Enlist the cooperation of parents/carers for this sort of arrangement.
- Try to raise self-esteem by pointing out achievements and using praise.
- Talk to his parents/carers about Peter's habit of putting objects into his pockets, but make absolutely sure that there is no doubt about what he is doing.
- Never 'search' Peter for lost objects or automatically assume that he has taken something that is missing.

CASE STUDY 10

Turn-taking

Sarah has a favourite toy and likes to play with this every day. Whenever there is a choice, she will monopolize the train set. If another child attempts to join her or even just to play alongside, she will respond by pushing the child away and become agitated if her space is invaded. Sarah will also refuse to wait her turn during games in small-group situations, often demanding to start first.

Possible reasons for this behaviour:

- Sarah feels insecure.
- She suffers from anxiety.
- She has an inability to empathize with others.
- She has been over-indulgenced/is used to getting own way at home, possibly the youngest/only child.
- She shows a lack of maturity.
- She may not have a train set at home and particularly likes it.
- She feels comfortable playing in that particular section of the pre-school.

Strategies:

- Temporarily remove the train set from the room.
- Encourage a short game with an adult, then one other child and an adult to model appropriate behaviour and gradually increase the group numbers.
- Give instant praise for appropriate behaviour.
- Use the train set as a reward – set aside special times for Sarah to play with the train.
- Clearly explain expectations on a session basis.
- Pair up with buddy role model.
- Use a visual prop to signal 'it's your turn' – only a child wearing the special tunic/hat/arm band can play with the train.

CASE STUDY 11

Autistic Spectrum Disorder

Michael seems withdrawn and appears to lack the ability to interact with others in the expected manner. He is mostly quiet and content to occupy himself with an activity of his own choosing, when he displays the ability to concentrate for long periods. He will scream in a high-pitched voice when he feels thwarted and will sometimes refuse to join an adult-led activity and will rock to and fro. When Michael is playing he will often make flapping movements with his hands. He dislikes the routine being changed and becomes distressed whenever this happens.

Possible reasons for this behaviour:

- He has had experience of trauma.
- There may be neglect in the home.
- He may be on the autistic spectrum.
- He may have a language disorder.

Strategies:

- Introduce a high degree of structure to the day.
- Use a personal, pictorial timetable for Michael.
- Take care to use unambiguous language.
- Give simple instructions accompanied by visual aids.
- Allow time for Michael to 'process' instructions.
- Use direct teaching of appropriate behaviours.
- Make clear rules and boundaries.
- Give very clear explanation of any changes to routine and assurances about when it will end, e.g. if going out for a walk always tell him that you will be coming back to the nursery/school.
- Ignore behaviours such as hand flapping or the insistence of wearing hats/hoods, etc. (if the behaviour is not hurting the child or others – ignore).

CASE STUDY 12

Aggression

Bhupinder likes to behave to her own agenda. She refuses to share equipment and monopolizes her favourite things. If another child approaches her at the sand tray, she often responds with verbal aggression and will throw sand into the child's face. She has a history of hitting other children and consequently they avoid contact with her.

Possible reasons for this behaviour:

- She is immature.
- She has poor language skills.
- There may be poor role models or experience of aggression in the home.
- She has a lack of experience in social skills.
- She has low self-esteem.

Strategies:

- Use personalized positive reinforcement every time appropriate behaviours are observed.
- Temporarily remove the sand tray.
- Use rules and consequences.
- Tactically ignore inappropriate behaviours.
- Model good and bad behaviour, e.g. with stories and puppets.
- Use a home-school contact book for positive comments.
- Involve the child in evaluating her own behaviour, e.g. use of smiley faces.

CASE STUDY 13

Spoiling others' work

Jack will often scribble all over the drawings of children nearby during art activities.

Possible reasons for this behaviour:

- Jack has low self-esteem and worries that other children's work is better than his own.
- He is attention-seeking and may enjoy the reaction of adults and children following this behaviour.
- He has a lack of social experiences.
- He has a lack of empathy with others.

Strategies:

- Raise self-esteem by highlighting achievements.
- Provide close supervision during drawing activities: talk to Jack about his picture and help him to stay focused.
- Allow him to change to a different activity as soon as he loses interest in drawing.
- Ignore negative behaviours.
- Pair up with an appropriate role model.
- Make expectations very clear.

CASE STUDY 14

Spoiling own work

After completing a drawing/painting Tracey will often scribble all over the picture with a black or red crayon.

Possible reasons for this behaviour:

- She may just enjoy the sensation of colouring over the picture.
- She is upset by home circumstances.
- She feels low self-esteem – she may feel that her work is not good enough.

Strategies:

- Check with parents/carers that this is her usual behaviour at home – ask them whether anything is worrying Tracey.
- Very prominently display a picture which has not been scribbled over, and praise her for it.
- If Tracey uses a lot of red or black colouring materials, ask parents/carers to check the possibility of colour blindness.
- Monitor closely and seek the help of an educational psychologist if the behaviour persists.

CASE STUDY 15

Using 'no'

Jordan has a strong temperament and enjoys pre-school when he can do activities he likes. If he is asked to go to a table-top activity he just keeps saying 'No, I won't go. You can't make me. I'll tell my mum,' over and over again. He will not move but just keeps saying the words.

Possible reasons for this behaviour:

- He has learnt the behaviour from home or elsewhere.
- He finds table-top activities difficult and is more confident in other areas.
- He likes to control, wants to have the last word.
- He has learnt that he will get his own way if he carries on for long enough.
- He feels insecure and this is his way of keeping a grip on things.

Strategies:

- Tactical ignoring – give no attention but immediately go to another child. It is important that Jordan is not allowed to carry on with other activities but has to stay in a set place until he is ready to join in the set activity – this will have to be planned by all staff.
- Give Jordan a restricted choice of activity: 'Do you want to do some cutting out on this table or play a matching game over on that table?'
- Continue with Jordan as if you have not heard, and gently lead him to the activity table.
- Use a timetable with Jordan so that he is aware of which activities he will need to do during the session – he can agree these and they can be recorded simply. He can cross out the activity as he completes it.
- Discuss with parents/carers so that similar ideas can be carried out at home if this is possible.
- Give praise whenever Jordan is doing what is expected.

CASE STUDY 16

Use of 'illness'

Gerry's parents have become very concerned as he is often sick before coming to pre-school. His parents still bring him and he usually settles. During the sessions he will often say he feels sick and rushes to the toilet and stays there for quite a long time on occasions. Gerry has been sent home in the past but his mother reports that he is fine as soon as he gets home.

Possible reasons for this behaviour:

- He is a highly anxious child who does not like change.
- Has there been a change of family circumstances such as a new baby?
- Gerry has learnt that if he says he feels sick, adults will give a high level of attention.
- There may be dietary problems, e.g. intolerance to certain foods.
- There may be medical reasons.
- Gerry finds it difficult to manage the complex social structure of a pre-school setting.
- He is very attached to his mother.
- Gerry may feel that his mother is upset and wants him to stay at home.

Strategies:

- Talk to Gerry about all the interesting things happening at the pre-school and encourage Mum to do the same before setting out from home.
- Recognize that Gerry may be a very anxious child and talk more with him about other children not wanting to leave their mother – he needs to be made aware that other children feel the same. Use stories/puppets.
- Provide Gerry with a key worker who greets him in the mornings and to whom he can go at any time during the session.
- Gerry may not have the language to express how he feels. It can be useful for adults to try to support him in verbalizing his thoughts by saying such things as 'I think you like to play here but like to be with your mum as well.' Both parents and pre-school staff need to give the same message and reassure Gerry that his worries will lessen each day.

- Check out any medical reasons for the difficulties.
- Consider whether he has difficulties in understanding what is said to him (receptive language problems).
- It is more helpful if pre-school staff can work out ways of keeping Gerry at pre-school rather than sending him home.

CASE STUDY 17

A 'runner'

Brandon is a lively boy and enjoys the big equipment and large space at the pre-school. He has worked out how to open the door and runs out of the large hall whenever possible. He also watches for staff as they open the door and will try to run out then.

Possible reasons for this behaviour:

- Brandon sees this as a game.
- He gets attention for doing this.
- He is curious about what is happening outside the hall.
- Brandon does not feel sufficiently 'confined' in such a large hall.
- He does this at home or elsewhere and he enjoys being chased by adults.
- Brandon is not ready for a full pre-school session.
- He is not sufficiently involved in/challenged by the activities on offer.

Strategies:

- Take Brandon on a tour of the building so that his curiosity is satisfied.
- Plan some special games and activities that will engage him.
- Give Brandon a high level of attention when he is focused on activities in the hall.
- Think about sectioning off the large hall into smaller areas if possible.
- Use going out of the large hall as a special reward for completing other activities – Brandon's reward could be to go for a five-minute walk outside the hall with an adult.
- Ask Brandon what he thinks might be outside of the hall and why he likes to go out.
- Discuss with parents/carers the possibility of shortening the session at pre-school until Brandon is ready for a longer session.
- Agree with parents/carers about what will happen when Brandon runs out.

CASE STUDY 18

Hiding

Chantelle is generally a quiet girl at nursery and seems to enjoy being there for most of the time. Members of staff are concerned as she hides under a table regularly, tucks herself in a corner and just stays there and will not come out.

Possible reasons for this behaviour:

- Chantelle finds the lively atmosphere too difficult.
- There are difficult circumstances at home that are upsetting her.
- She gets tired quickly.
- She needs time for personal space.
- She needs the security of a smaller, more comforting area.

Strategies:

- Give Chantelle a special quiet place to go in the nursery or allow her to sit/lie on a cushion under the table.
- Discuss with parents/carers whether they know why this is happening – does this happen at home?
- Encourage her to have a buddy who will sit with her in a quiet area.
- Think about the structure of the session – are there enough quiet times or quiet areas where Chantelle can go?
- Organize a timetable for Chantelle so that there are opportunities for her to have a quiet time during the sessions.

CASE STUDY 19

Self injuries

Tariq is a mischievous little boy and generally likes to join in with most pre-school activities. On occasions he just will not join in and will head-butt against the wall or the floor if staff try to encourage him to join in.

Possible reasons for this behaviour:

- Tariq does not like to join in with specific activities.
- He has not learnt a more appropriate way of saying he does not want to join in at that time.
- He may be experiencing some pain, such as earache, or there may be another medical reason.
- He has learnt that this method will get him his own way at home.

Strategies:

- Identify the 'trigger points' for this behaviour and consider whether they can be avoided.
- Tariq will need to be taught alternative ways of saying he does not wish to do something – it may be helpful for staff to verbalize how they think he is feeling, saying something like, 'I think that it makes you feel angry/annoyed/cross when I ask you to sit at the art table.'
- Tactical ignoring. Ensure that Tariq cannot hurt himself – he should be placed in an area with cushions while staff observe him from a distance.
- Provide visual communication cards to help him communicate how he is feeling (simple illustration).
- Ask parent/carers to check out any medical reasons if that is felt to be a useful route.
- Tariq will require a lot of praise when he is doing things well.
- Although it can be very frightening for adults to watch, most children who use this tactic as a method of control know their limits and will not seriously hurt themselves.

CASE STUDY 20

Swearing

Storm has recently started at pre-school and constantly swears at staff and children. This swearing can last several minutes and be highly repetitive. Storm does not speak very much apart from the swearing.

Possible reasons for this behaviour:

- Storm has learnt vocabulary from home or elsewhere.
- She is not aware of the social inappropriateness of such language.
- She may get attention at home for swearing and continues with that in the pre-school.
- Language disorder and difficulty, e.g. Tourette's syndrome or neurological problems (this is rare).
- She may use swear words at home if she does not want to do something.

Strategies:

- Storm may need to be taught alternative words to use at pre-school – she could practise this through role-play with other children.
- It might be helpful to talk to parents/carers to clarify where she could have learnt the words and suggest that alternative words are used at home.
- Storm may benefit from a speech and language programme if her general vocabulary is very restricted.
- Storm may need opportunities to express her feelings through role-play, puppets or a visual communication system.

CASE STUDY 21

Undressing

All of a sudden Kayleigh will start to take her clothes off at pre-school. She seems totally oblivious of children and adults when she does this and just stands there.

Possible reasons for this behaviour:

- She likes the sensation of wearing no clothes.
- She feels hot.
- She gets adult attention for doing this.
- She has social communication difficulties – not understanding socially acceptable norms.
- She doesn't want to be in the situation.

Strategies:

- Explain to Kayleigh that there are certain times to undress (bed-time, swimming, bathing, PE, etc.) – and other times when it is not appropriate. Use a doll to demonstrate, and let her dress and undress the doll.
- Use clothes that are more difficult to remove, e.g. dungarees.
- Suggest she should wear very lightweight clothes.
- Have available a PE kit, shorts and T-shirt for her to change into if she starts to undress.
- Distract Kayleigh as soon as someone notices, and encourage her to do something else.
- Give her lots of praise for looking nice in her clothes.

CASE STUDY 22

Spitting

Aiden has started to spit a lot at pre-school. He will either spit on his own or will spit at adults or other children.

Possible reasons for this behaviour:

- He is intrigued by the bodily function.
- He recognizes that he gets a response.
- He likes to get noticed.
- He is imitating the behaviour of other people he sees.
- There has been a change of family circumstances.
- There may be a medical reason.

Strategies:

- Explain to Aiden that spitting is not acceptable – if he wants to spit he needs to go into a specified place away from others and spit into a tissue.
- Praise Aiden for playing nicely and reinforce all good behaviours.
- Ask Aiden why he spits.
- Check with parents/carers whether this is happening at home or elsewhere.
- Suggest a check-up with the doctor.

CASE STUDY 23

Over affection

Lauren often goes straight up to adults, even adults she does not know, and gives them a big hug. She does this constantly and without discrimination. She not only hugs them but will not let go and tries to climb onto their laps if given the opportunity. She also does this to children and has caused some children to complain to an adult.

Possible reasons for this behaviour:

- Lauren needs attention.
- She comes from a very affectionate family.
- She has a limited family or social circle.
- She has the desire to remain younger than her chronological age.
- She doesn't realize that this behaviour is not appropriate in the pre-school setting.
- Lauren has autistic tendencies.

Strategies:

- Explain to Lauren that this is not acceptable behaviour because some people do not like to be hugged all the time – this may need careful explanation because she may be quite vulnerable if she is apt to go to strangers and exhibit this behaviour.
- Give Lauren appropriate levels of attention.
- Give alternatives, e.g. a teddy to cuddle.
- Praise Lauren when she exhibits independent behaviours.

CASE STUDY 24

Lying

Ben always denies he has done something even if an adult has observed him. Sometimes he makes up stories that at the time seem very plausible. Whenever Ben is seen doing something such as pushing or hitting another child, his first response will be 'I didn't do it' and perhaps even to make something up about one of his peers.

Possible reasons for this behaviour:

- He is attention-seeking.
- There is a lack of consistency in his management.
- He suffers from anxiety.
- He may do this as a retreat from the real world.

Strategies:

- Ensure a consistent approach from pre-school staff and, if possible, from parents/carers.
- Make a firm statement of the facts and be accurate: 'I saw you throw the building block and it hit Ashley on the head,' not 'I saw you throw the block at Ashley.'
- Condemn the behaviour, not the child: 'That isn't a nice thing to do,' not 'You are not a nice person/you are a naughty boy.'
- Always give him a way out so that he is not afraid to 'own up': 'I'm sure you didn't mean to hurt Ashley, so say you're sorry and try not to do it again.'
- Don't have any prolonged arguing or explanations from adults.
- Monitor closely – try to divert Ben when he looks as though he is going to lie by providing a true version of events with which he can agree.
- Use stories to model honest behaviour.
- Record serious incidents.

CASE STUDY 25

'First'

Charlie always has to be first to start a game. He will push other children out of the way in his rush to be at the front of a line, and becomes difficult if he cannot get his own way.

Possible reasons for this behaviour:

- Charlie likes attention.
- He likes to control adults.
- He has low self-esteem.
- He lacks social awareness.
- He has a possible social communication disorder.

Strategies:

- Give praise for appropriate behaviour.
- Give Charlie a special job to distract him, e.g. holding the door.
- Place Charlie next to a buddy in the line.
- Change Charlie's place in the line regularly so that he gets used to being in different places. Give the children numbers, then instructions: 'all the ones line up, all the twos' or 'everyone wearing . . .'
- Do the children have to line up? It might be worth considering alternative methods of travelling around the building.

CASE STUDY 26

Biting

Jasmine often resorts to biting other children when she cannot get her own way or whenever she feels that things are not going her way. She has even bitten adults in the setting and often refuses to say sorry.

Possible reasons for this behaviour:

- She has a poor vocabulary – she does not possess the verbal skills to express herself.
- Jasmine may be at an early developmental stage and the biting could just be a reflection of her general development and cognitive abilities – she will need to be treated accordingly. Planning may need adjusting to take her developmental needs into account.
- She has an inability to control her feelings, especially those of anger.
- Jasmine has learnt that whenever she does this she gets her own way.
- It is an attempt to increase her status and/or power within the family hierarchy.
- There has been inconsistent management at home.

Strategies:

- Whenever Jasmine bites, staff should immediately pay attention to the child who has been bitten while initially ignoring Jasmine.
- Jasmine must be told in a very explicit and concise manner that biting will not be tolerated.
- Staff may need to plan very carefully for Jasmine after observing and gathering information about her developmental stage.
- She should have the opportunity to engage with a small group of children regularly in an adult-led activity while appropriate behaviours are modelled.
- Praise should be given whenever Jasmine is able to resolve conflicts without resorting to biting.
- When an incident of biting occurs, staff should always talk to both parents/carers.
- It would be a good idea to implement a management plan for any such incidents and agree this with parents/carers.

CASE STUDY 27

Refusal to stop playing a game on an electronic device

Finley arrives happily into the pre-school and usually joins in readily alongside others at the sand or water play. However, once he has access to one of the setting's tablet devices which is set up with simple jigsaw or matching games, he loudly and sometimes violently refuses to move on to anything else. On one occasion he threw the device to the floor and ran off to the soft play area and sobbed.

Possible reasons for this behaviour:

- They may have free access to a tablet device at home and have become over-reliant on its use.
- They find communicating with others challenging and prefer playing on their own.
- They do not find the other activities available as interesting as the device.

Strategies:

- Ensure adequate time is allowed for a game to finish and a warning given that time will be up in, say one or two minutes (and stick to it).
- Make it clear from the start to children and adults that the use of electronic devices in the pre-school is time-limited (an egg-timer on the device itself as well as a real sand-timer might help).
- Use a visual timetable to demonstrate that moving on to another activity is expected and applies to everyone.
- Ensure that there are some really interesting activities nearby to tempt them away from the device.
- Find a 'buddy' who will encourage play and interaction.
- Check with the parent/carer whether the child behaves similarly at home (and whether they are allowed unlimited use).
- Consider having a device-free day in the setting.

CASE STUDY 28

Fear of people and animals

Peter is a four-year-old boy who has not attended a nursery because of his fear of people other than his mother and grandmother. Peter insists on wearing a baseball cap that he pulls down over his eyes so that he cannot see faces and so that he can avoid eye contact.

When Peter's mother tries to take him out for routine events like shopping or using public transport, he reacts by resisting any attempts to make him board a bus or enter a shop. Peter cries, screams and struggles to such an extent that his mother usually takes him home. Peter's difficulties are impacting significantly upon family life, which to all intents and purposes is confined to the home.

Peter ignores all interactions from people other than his mother and grandmother. When Peter speaks to his mother, his speech is unintelligible and he uses gesture to make his needs and wants clear to her.

Peter likes to stick to the same routines every day and demonstrates inflexibility at home with regard to the food he will eat and the toys he likes to play with. Peter's mother has had to re-home the family dog due to his inability to tolerate being in the same room as the pet.

Possible reasons for this behaviour:

- Peter has a genuine fear of people and animals.
- Peter has discovered he is able to control his life by the use of the above behaviours.
- Peter may have difficulties that could be associated with the autistic spectrum.

Strategies:

- Peter should be referred to a consultant paediatrician for a developmental assessment.
- Peter's mother should be encouraged and helped to find a suitable nursery/pre-school so that assessments can be made about any possible educational difficulties.
- If possible, the nursery should be assisted with a gentle transition between home and nursery so that Peter is helped to settle into the new environment.

- Peter's mother should consider using visual methods of showing him what will happen – visual time line or timetable of events – and including changes to his routine.
- At first, Peter's mother should be encouraged to stay at the nursery and then to leave him for a short time, gradually leaving him for longer so that an hour per day is achieved.
- If at all possible, the nursery should provide a key worker who will assist Peter with settling in, providing visual cue cards for points of reference/routines, and with making the transition to using a visual timetable. The visual timetable should always include a picture of home time and Peter's mother collecting him.
- After this, depending upon how successfully Peter accepts the situation, he should be left for a whole session.
- Staff should always use a highly visual method of communicating with Peter and this should include pictures, cue cards and perhaps signing to accompany speech.
- Peter should be encouraged to make choices (from a maximum of two items) and adults should model appropriate language.
- Language models may begin with a single word and then by linking a noun and a verb e.g. 'eat biscuit', 'play car'.
- Peter should be monitored closely to assess the level of his difficulties, with the appropriate outside agencies being involved.
- Peter should be referred to a speech and language therapist.
- Peter should be referred to a dietician.
- Educational agencies should be involved to assess his likely needs upon school entry.

Note:

The above case study is a description of true events with obvious alterations to avoid identification. 'Peter' was successfully integrated into a nursery and now attends for five sessions independently. He was hesitant at first, but demonstrated a real (and surprising) willingness to take part in activities and use toys and equipment, especially the large, well-equipped outdoor play area. At first, Peter kept his baseball cap pulled low down over his eyes. The staff were very willing to help with a slow and gradual transition and were able to provide an assistant who now supports with 'light touch' and prompting when necessary. Peter uses a visual timetable and is able to make choices using picture cards often accompanied by a single word. Peter has stopped wearing his baseball cap and uses eye contact on his own terms. Peter plays alongside children, tolerating their presence, and responds to adult direction very well. Peter demonstrates good cognitive abilities and is able to count to at least 50, is able to problem-solve, is able to tell the time, and is able to carry out simple functions with numbers. His learning profile is typically uneven for children with his level of difficulty. Peter has been diagnosed with Autistic Spectrum Disorder and is on the waiting list for a place in a special unit for children with ASD.

CASE STUDY 29

Eating objects

Sarah is four years old and has attended the same nursery since she was three.

Sarah eats items such as fluff from the carpet, foam rubber, wool, play dough, uncooked pasta, paint, cake and bread mix, snacks that belong to other children, egg shells, leaves and other assorted items.

Sarah demonstrates this behaviour on a daily basis and appears to ignore all instructions not to do this. Staff at her nursery are concerned that she will eat something that will eventually make her ill.

In all other respects, Sarah's behaviour appears to be age-appropriate.

Possible reasons for this behaviour:

- Sarah has a sensory need that requires assessment.
- Sarah could be suffering from a deficiency in her diet and she is demonstrating an urge to satisfy this.
- Sarah is developmentally delayed.

Strategies:

- Refer Sarah for a sensory assessment.
- The sensory assessment may throw up issues that can be addressed at home and at school.
- Draw up a care plan for Sarah so all staff are aware of the difficulty and how to manage it.
- Refer Sarah to the paediatrician for a medical assessment to rule out possible dietary issues.
- Provide Sarah with a pictorial timetable that includes snack times.
- Provide Sarah with supervision at snack times and make sure that she eats appropriate things at that time.
- Allow Sarah to remove the 'snack picture' and to put it into a 'finished box'.
- Provide Sarah with a visual representation of things she is allowed to eat and things that are not for eating and encourage her to 'sort' into categories.
- Sarah may need a special sensory 'kit' that includes items she can chew safely.

CASE STUDY 30

Falling asleep

Daniel is nearly four years old and has attended a pre-school for about nine months. When he comes into pre-school, he goes straight to the home corner, curls up on an armchair and appears to go to sleep.

When not asleep, Daniel remains either on the chair or on the mat nearby and observes the activity in the pre-school room. He does not interact with other children and only interacts with adults if they ask a direct question, answering with a single word or a nod.

Possible reasons for this behaviour:

- Daniel has an illness that requires investigation.
- Daniel is suffering emotional distress.
- Daniel may be on the autistic spectrum.
- Daniel is suffering abuse.

Strategies:

- Daniel should be referred to a paediatrician for a full developmental assessment.
- The staff should arrange a meeting with parents to assess whether this behaviour is the norm at home as well as in the pre-school.
- If Daniel has a typical pattern of waking and sleeping at home, efforts should be made to assess whether Daniel finds the environment stressful and resorts to sleep in order to escape from any discomfort.
- Staff should make the physical environment as stress-free as possible.
- Provide a 'retreat' such as a tent or an area that is screened from the general busy areas in the pre-school room.
- Provide Daniel with a pictorial timetable of the session that includes times when he is allowed to use the 'retreat'.
- During other times, structure Daniel's session so that he knows exactly what he will be doing, and equipment and materials he needs for painting, etc. should also be included on the timetable.
- Depending upon the outcome of the paediatrician's assessment, staff should monitor any effect the strategies have upon Daniel's ability to remain awake and to improve progress with social interaction.
- If speech, language and social interaction remain limited, staff should use a highly visual method of communicating with Daniel.
- A diary may be useful to record any patterns of sleeping/waking.

CASE STUDY 31

Oppositional, violent behaviours

Donna is a four-year-old girl who has been asked to leave three previous pre-schools for constant defiance and aggression. Donna's behaviour is a cause for concern and she also has some difficulty with speech sound production, thus making her speech slightly difficult to understand.

Donna behaves to her own agenda and refuses to cooperate with even simple instructions to sit and listen to a story or to join a small group of children engaged in a task. Donna responds to unwanted interactions from adults by hitting out at them.

Donna lashes out at other children at random, refuses to share toys and refuses to take turns. Donna likes to have her own way, and bites, hits and scratches other children if they assert themselves.

Staff are at a loss as to how they should tackle Donna, as she behaves to her own agenda from the moment she arrives in the morning and for the duration of the session. Parents of other children are making complaints about bruises and bite marks.

Possible reasons for this behaviour:

- Donna has learnt that using aggression is a successful way of getting what she wants.
- Donna has a language disorder.
- Donna has a specific behavioural disorder.
- Donna has never been exposed to boundaries regarding behaviour.

Strategies:

- Steps should be taken to rule out any medical reason for Donna's behaviour.
- An assessment of Donna's speech and language skills should be sought.
- Donna's behaviour should be addressed as a matter of priority.
- A Behaviour Plan should be implemented.
- The plan should highlight behaviours that are not acceptable and the sanctions that will take place as a result.
- The plan should also highlight rewards that will be used for wanted behaviours.
- Avoid using Donna's name when interacting with her over unwanted behaviours, and use her name when staff catch her demonstrating acceptable or wanted behaviours.

- The rewards should be given for wanted behaviours every time at first and could include stickers, praise, time with a favourite toy.
- The Plan should outline how staff will respond to target behaviours so that complete consistency can be maintained.
- Socially unacceptable behaviours like hitting, biting, etc. should never be ignored and should be dealt with swiftly by implementing sanctions agreed on the Behaviour Plan.
- If 'time out' is to be used as a sanction, this should involve no attention or eye contact from adults. Time out – one minute for every year of the child's life.
- Avoid explanations but stick to the points outlined in the Behaviour Plan, thereby putting the responsibility for the behaviour firmly with Donna.
- The plan should be discussed and agreed with parents so that management can be consistent between home and pre-school.
- A high degree of structure to the session should be imposed upon Donna at first. Choices should be limited at first and then gradually extended in line with Donna's ability to progress.
- A visual timetable of Donna's session should be implemented.
- Donna's session should be shortened at first and if possible, she should be allowed to come into pre-school 15 minutes before all the other children arrive.
- A staff member should go over the timetable with Donna during this time and also go over the Behaviour Plan upon admittance.
- The staff member should supervise Donna closely at first and make sure that she sticks to activities on her visual timetable.
- Gradually, allow Donna a degree of choice regarding activities, but she must stick to these and must complete at least one task directed by an adult.
- Parents should make sure that they arrive at the pre-school at the agreed time and also that they collect Donna when agreed.
- Donna's session should be gradually lengthened depending upon success and the aim should be to integrate her into the full session over time.
- A home-school contact book should be implemented for positive achievements and comments only. This should go back and forth between home and school so that Donna can talk about things she has done well in both settings.
- Give Donna responsibility.
- The general strategy should be viewed as long-term. Behaviours that are entrenched can take a relatively long period to change. Consistency is important.

CASE STUDY 32

Extreme emotional responses

Ben is a four-year-old child with a stable family background and has attended the same pre-school for nearly two years.

Ben is a very intelligent child with a wide vocabulary and good speech, language and communication skills.

Ben reacts to routine events like being asked to play with a different toy/s by becoming extremely distressed and crying in an almost melodramatic fashion.

Sometimes he walks up and down the room repetitively, mumbling to himself and clutching his head in a despairing manner. Ben's outbursts are out of all proportion to the actual event.

It takes staff a considerable period of time to help Ben regain composure after these episodes.

Ben takes part in activities as long as he thinks he can succeed; if he begins to 'fail' in his opinion, he withdraws. During small-group activities/games, Ben only joins in if he can maintain some control over the situation – if not, he withdraws. Ben demonstrates a general lack of awareness of social situations and tends to interact with specific children and adults only.

Ben is inflexible and likes to use props that are carried around with him all day, e.g. a small model of Thomas the Tank Engine.

Ben has extreme difficulty understanding the point of view of others. He demonstrates obsessional behaviours and plays with a limited range of things.

Ben is achieving at age-appropriate levels with the Early Years Foundation Stage Curriculum and is functioning in advance of peers in some areas.

Possible reasons for this behaviour:

- Ben is an intelligent child and has realized that some behaviours result in getting what he wants.
- Ben has issues that could be categorized as 'high-functioning' autistic difficulties.
- Ben has speech and language difficulties.

Strategies:

- Staff should gather information about Ben's behaviour and share their concerns with parents in the first instance.

- Ben should be referred to a paediatrician.
- If the outcome of the paediatric assessment results in a diagnosis of ASD the setting should consider implementing some basic managing strategies.
- A behaviour management plan should be implemented so that staff react to outbursts with consistency.
- A personal, visual timetable of the session should be implemented and a high degree of structure should be imposed.
- Ben should be encouraged to stick activities on the timetable and carry these out in order.
- One-to-one working should be included on the timetable.
- During these sessions the following activities can be considered:
  a) identifying emotions from photographs;
  b) asking 'why' questions about pictures of children who are demonstrating emotions;
  c) telling of social stories to encourage thinking about appropriate responses;
  d) sequencing events;
  e) predicting the outcome/ending of a story by using the words 'what CAN happen . . .';
  f) turn-taking games that have to be completed using a visual method of measuring the time.
- Ben should be encouraged to view his paintings, drawings, models, etc. with a positive attitude, and adults should praise his efforts and help him to realize that it is quite acceptable if things are not 'perfect'. Examples of children's work could be used in small-group situations to highlight positive aspects of the drawings/paintings/models.
- Ben will benefit from help to develop coping structures and strategies that he can rely upon for developing independence.
- Ben may benefit from a notebook that has information about materials and resources he needs for various activities.
- This can be extended to helping with transition from pre-school to school.

ASD and speech and language disorder

Children who are attending pre-provisions, nurseries and foundation units and who may or may not have a diagnosis of ASD demonstrate behaviours that are usually described as a 'triad of impairment' in the following areas: speech, language and communication, social interaction and repetitive/stereotypical behaviours. However, as with all children, children with ASD present as unique individuals and in order to manage their difficulties, practitioners will have to 'tailor' strategies to suit rather than using a blanket approach to manage behaviours effectively. In general children with ASD or with speech and language disorders benefit from a highly visual and structured approach to teaching and learning. The following case studies are an attempt to show that although children may have the same diagnosis, strategies should reflect individual needs.

Children with diagnosis of speech and language disorders demonstrate behaviours that can be likened to the behaviours seen in children with an ASD diagnosis. It is the job of an educationalist to identify the primary need and to address this, in partnership with involved professionals and parents, with targeted support. It is important to be consistent, and strategies that work will need to be employed at home and at school for best results.

CASE STUDY 33

Leo, four years old, a child with a diagnosis of ASD

Leo uses complete and grammatically correct sentences to communicate with adults. He has a wide vocabulary and likes to talk to visiting adults as well as staff in his nursery. Leo uses eye contact on his own terms especially when interest levels are high or when he wants something. Leo will sometimes use prolonged eye contact and put his face very close to that of the person he is speaking to. If adults ask Leo a direct question, he is able to supply the correct answer straight away. If he is asked an open-ended question or a 'why' question, Leo will usually ignore this or repeat it. Sometimes, perhaps even an hour later, Leo will 'answer' the question out of context without checking to see whether the relevant adult is nearby. He uses learnt jargon or phrases that are not directed to any particular person. Leo is judged to be an able child and is doing very well with the curriculum, being ahead of peers in subjects like mathematical knowledge. However, he becomes very distressed if the routines are changed and if his own notion of what he will be doing during the session is disrupted in any way.

Leo does not interact with peers socially, and prefers to remain on the sidelines of groups although he has recently started to play with one particular child in the setting. Leo puts his hands over his ears frequently during the session.

He likes to play repetitively with a limited range of equipment, usually train tracks or cars.

Leo has no concept of time and will use 'yesterday', 'tomorrow', 'before' and 'after' out of context or inappropriately.

Strategies:

- Implement a high degree of structure to Leo's sessions.
- Implement a visual timetable of Leo's session and break this down into manageable 'chunks'.
- Leo's timetable should preferably run from left to right (rather than top to bottom) and might include arrows to show the direction of 'travel'.
- Always include 'home time'.
- Be very aware that although Leo appears to have good levels of language skills, he may have difficulty understanding more complex language and may require extended time to process this and/or extra visual help to do this. For example, Leo may need a

personal copy of the book at story time and an adult to point to key characters/events to aid comprehension.

- Use the vocabulary 'first', 'next', 'last', 'yesterday', 'today', 'tomorrow' to reinforce time concepts along with visual clues on the timetable.
- Provide daily opportunities when Leo arrives for a key worker to discuss the timetable and include any changes to the routine.
- Use frequent verbal/visual reminders about the change. Accompany verbal instructions with visual aids or signs whenever possible.
- Provide 'time out' or a refuge for Leo for when he becomes distressed.
- Provide a place of calm in order to balance any distress caused by sensory overload.
- Use targeted support sessions to work on Leo's receptive language skills, e.g. explore whether he understands the use of positional language and also his understanding of complex instructions.
- Use targeted support to explore whether Leo is able to sequence a set of picture cards and whether he can express what is happening.
- Assess whether Leo is able to supply the ending to a familiar repetitive story.
- Assess whether Leo is able to supply the ending to an unfamiliar story.
- Assess Leo's ability to respond to 'why' and 'how' questions and provide opportunities for language modelling.
- Staff may need to consider whether the physical environment can be adapted to accommodate any sensory issues that affect Leo.
- The ongoing input of a speech and language therapist will be useful for planning programmes of work designed to develop Leo's ability to understand and to express language effectively.

CASE STUDY 34

Rachel, four years old, a child with a diagnosis of ASD

Rachel has attended her nursery for over a year and rarely makes eye contact with either adults or children. Rachel uses pointing and gesture in order to indicate need, and sometimes copies a modelled single word. Rachel requires adults to guide her to an activity, without which she would play with the building bricks repetitively by emptying the box they are kept in and then filling it up again. Rachel does not respond to her name being called and does not join in with group activities like singing or doing actions to stories/ hymes. She pushes other children away if they get too close to her or try to join her in play. Rachel is not toilet trained and shows no awareness of being uncomfortable. Rachel has no sense of danger and an increased pain threshold.

Strategies:

- Rachel has a significant level of need and will require specialist teaching in order to make progress.
- In the nursery, staff should use a highly visual method of communicating with Rachel.
- Staff should use reduced language when addressing Rachel.
- Rachel should be taught to respond to visual cue cards, especially 'stop' for keeping her safe. For example, adults may have to intervene physically if Rachel attempts to do anything that could lead her to hurt herself – this action should be accompanied by a visual sign for 'stop'.
- Other visual aids such as 'good looking', 'good sitting', 'good listening' should be employed regularly.
- Visual cue cards should be made for points of reference and for routine events.
- Rachel should be provided with her own personal cushion for joining group activities.
- Actions to songs, etc. should be modelled by an adult and Rachel should be assisted to participate via close adult support.
- Rachel should be encouraged to make choices. Adults should offer a maximum of two items and model language for Rachel to copy at first. This should be extended to linking a noun and a verb, e.g. 'drink milk', and modelled for Rachel to copy.

- She may require a visual method of making choices depending upon progress by being presented with visual representations of what is on offer, picture cards or photos.
- Rachel should be encouraged to follow simple instruction, e.g. 'get coat' accompanied by a visual aid. Adults should stick to using key words and only give one instruction at a time.
- She may benefit from being taught signing.
- Rachel will benefit from the use of photographs of herself in the nursery carrying out routine events.
- She will require adults to model play and to use language modelling to accompany this.
- Rachel will require the ongoing input of a speech and language therapist for programmes of work to develop her ability to communicate.
- Rachel may benefit from a sensory assessment.

CASE STUDY 35

Liam, four years old, a child with a diagnosis of ASD

Liam has attended nursery for over a year. He has always been viewed by staff as a very emotional child with exaggerated responses to daily events. Staff have no concerns about Liam's ability to understand even complex ideas and instructions, and describe his use of language as 'excellent'. He uses well-constructed sentences, is able to hold conversations with adults and to describe stories, outings and to predict outcomes with age-appropriate language skills. Liam's progress with the Early Years Foundation Stage Curriculum is age-appropriate or even in advance of peers.

Liam responds with extreme emotion, throwing himself on the floor, wailing and sobbing if not allowed to play with his favourite toy. He has an obsessional interest in trains, Thomas the Tank Engine in particular. He holds a model train at all times, taking it everywhere with him. Liam is extremely inflexible, demanding that the same route is followed home, to nursery, to the shops and that the same routines are adhered to in the home. Liam appears to be unable to recognize when people are sad, happy or angry. He appears unable to accept that drawings/paintings that he considers 'wrong' are quite acceptable and are valued by staff and parents. If he thinks that he has done something incorrectly, he will respond with heightened emotion, crying and flinging himself onto the floor. When asked to join in with small-group games, Liam often plays for a short time before withdrawing if he cannot control the outcome. Liam's mother reports that he is often rude to strangers in the street or shops without warning. He uses echolalia and demonstrates word finding difficulties on an inconsistent basis. When he cannot think of the exact word he wants, Liam becomes emotionally distressed. Staff and parents are concerned about how Liam will cope with transferring to school.

Strategies:

- Liam may benefit from a full language assessment from a speech and language therapist even though he appears to have good verbal skills.
- The assessment may indicate possible processing difficulties.
- Liam will benefit from a visual timetable of daily events. Changes to the routine should be included and he should be given frequent verbal reminders about the change.

- A structure to 'unstructured' times of the day like 'tidy up' or transition times of the day should be planned for Liam to rely upon, for example he will need photos of himself lining up or tidying up.
- Liam should be introduced to a personal method of coping with perceived 'failure'. For example, he should be shown different outcomes to painting or drawing and encouraged to describe how 'good' they are.
- Liam should be exposed to photographs of faces showing a range of emotions, and assessments should be made about whether he is able to identify these.
- Social stories could be used in order to highlight the difference between trivial and significant events and the way in which people respond to these.
- Social skills groups could be used to reinforce appropriate social responses to a range of situations.
- Liam would benefit from regular small-group activities to practise turn-taking and cooperative social interaction skills.
- Staff may need to consider whether the physical environment is suitable from a sensory point of view.
- Liam may benefit from 'time out' or a refuge to help him to calm down when distress levels are high.
- He will benefit from an extended 'transition' period to school. Staff will need to make contact with the receiving school and plan a more intensive transition package into school. Liam will require a visual representation of school transition on his timetable. More visits than usual should be planned to the receiving school. At home, Liam should be encouraged to put his school uniform on and take the route to his new school well before the beginning of the term. He should practise putting his PE kit on and getting dressed again so that he is independent. He may require a sequential picture reminder of how to do this.
- Strategies to help Liam to cope with moderating his emotional responses should involve making him dependent upon a set of personal coping mechanisms rather than being dependent upon key workers and other adults. Liam will encounter many adults during his school career and unfortunately this could result in inconsistencies in management.
- In future, consideration will have to be given to strategies that help Liam with collecting the right materials and resources for different subject lessons. A personal notebook with timetables, equipment needed for lessons, etc. will help to reduce stress levels.

- Liam may benefit from a 'transition' area that he can access to check his timetable, check what equipment is needed and perhaps a 'workstation' that is set up with a structure and a format for beginning and completing a task. The workstation may be a booth or a screened area depending upon need.
- Emphasis should be placed upon providing an educational environment that is planned and organized to reduce possible raising of stress levels.

CASE STUDY 36

Jake

Jake was the first baby in the family and was given constant attention by various family members for his first two years. Jake's mum then went back to work and Jake attended the local day nursery. There had been a gradual part-time introduction to nursery staff and routine and Jake's mum ensured he seemed happy at nursery before returning to work. Jake had an allocated caseworker whom he looked forward to seeing each morning.

Jake appeared to settle for the first week but then kept asking people 'When go home?' and they kept telling him it was time for play and lunch and afternoon rest first. He did not appear to be satisfied with this and kept repeating the question and becoming more agitated, waiting as near to the door as he could.

Possible reasons for this behaviour:

- Jake does not yet understand the concept of time.
- Jake does not understand the language and words said to him.
- Jake may find something disturbing at the nursery.

Strategies:

- Maintain close observation to try to determine whether there are specific times or conditions that are upsetting Jake. He may be getting overtired and may need an extra nap.
- It may be helpful to have a picture board of the pattern of the day. Jake can take down the cards as the activities are complete. This will give Jake a clear idea of the pattern to the day and he should be able to look at the board so that a routine is established. Photographs could be useful.
- Use very clear vocabulary so that Jake associates the words with the pictures or photographs so that he will gradually become less reliant on the daily planner.

CASE STUDY 37

Rosie

Rosie started pre-school at two and a half years. Her mum told the pre-school that she was 'quite hard work' at home and had started to become more difficult.

Pre-school staff soon noticed that Rosie would sneakily take other children's toys and if they were taken away from her either by staff or by another child she would lie on the floor and kick and scream. She would keep this up for about half an hour and would kick any person who came near her. This was mentioned to Rosie's mum who said that this was not typical of Rosie's behaviour at home, although she did scream if she didn't get what she wanted. Rosie's mum said she did not always give in to her.

Possible reasons for this behaviour:

- Rosie is getting mixed messages from her mother's response to her behaviour.
- Rosie is finding it more difficult to share with other children.
- Rosie feels she may eventually get what she wants at nursery if she screams long enough, as this is the way it often works at home. Rosie's behaviour is becoming more and more exaggerated as this has not currently worked for her.

Strategies:

- The only way to make it clear to Rosie that this behaviour will not be tolerated is to consistently maintain the rule that snatching is not allowed. This may take several weeks. It will be important to ensure that Rosie will not hurt herself and to move the other children away from her until she has calmed down. If possible, Rosie should be encouraged to go into a specific 'calming corner' on her own where she has specific toys to play with or cloth books that she cannot tear up. If possible play some soothing music in that area to enable her to calm down.
- Rosie could be encouraged or taught to play with toys with other children, one child to begin with and an adult present.
- It may be useful to discuss Rosie's behaviour with her mother so that she is clear about the consistent rules in the pre-school. Rosie's mother should be encouraged to also be clear and consistent about boundaries if possible. There could be a contact book between home and pre-school where Rosie gets a star or special sticker for every time she follows the rules set.

CASE STUDY 38

Frankie

Frankie had been at pre-school since she was a baby and appeared to have settled in well. When she was nearly two years old she started to bite the other children at pre-school, including the very young children who were just crawling. Children became very frightened of being near her. She even bit the adults who tried to come near her to stop her. Scolding or moving her away from the situation did not deter her at the next opportunity she got. Staff became very anxious.

Possible reasons for this behaviour:

- Frankie saw that she got a reaction whenever she bit anyone. It is possible that the focus was on younger children in the pre-school and less on her so she started to demand attention in the most effective way she was able at the time.
- Frankie may find biting an effective way of getting what she wants at home.
- Frankie may use biting as a way of showing her frustration.

Strategies:

- A very effective way of helping Frankie is to buy a special wrist band that can be chewed. Frankie should be encouraged to use the wrist band whenever she shows signs of attempting to bite others.
- Frankie could be given her own special toys to bite when she wants to bite someone.
- This should be discussed with Frankie's parents/carers and they could be asked to record when the biting happens at home. This should also happen at pre-school, and a behavioural support plan could be devised.
- Frankie may have additional difficulties so it would be advisable to keep a record of her behaviour, observe which toys she chooses to play with, and seek further support if this continues.

CASE STUDY 39

JT

JT came into pre-school like a tornado. He was about two years old and immediately knocked anything he could off the shelving, threw all the books out of the bookcase and started to try to pull toys apart. He seemed oblivious of others and did not notice their disapproving looks or even when staff told him not to do that. His mother was in such a position that she needed to work and just left him each morning, coming back each evening to a catalogue of problems.

Possible reasons for this behaviour:

- JT is totally fascinated by seeing how things work and likes to see what happens when he knocks this over, etc.
- JT may have ADHD (Attention Deficit Hyperactivity Disorder) or autism, although these disorders are truly difficult to diagnose until the child is much older.
- Boys are generally more physical in their play, which needs to be appropriately channelled.
- JT engages in this behaviour at home and has no boundaries set.
- JT has language and understanding difficulties.

Strategies:

- JT should be shown how to behave for specific parts of the day, e.g. a picture timetable for when he comes into the pre-school.
- A specific caseworker allocated to JT should collect him from outside the pre-school and spend individual time with him.
- Calm music could be played as a background in the pre-school. Research has shown that soft background music can reduce noise level and unwanted behaviour.
- Ensure JT's mother is clear about how he is expected to behave in pre-school and encourage her to reward JT for good behaviour at home. Rewards should also be given at pre-school.
- JT may need to be given a more physical activity as soon as he enters pre-school such as a sit on toy he can drive around. A clear physical programme may need to be designed for him.

SECTION 4

Managing the environment (including the role of the teaching assistant)

The space

Display and learning resources

Managing staff

Communicating

General good practice strategies

Strategies for children with behavioural difficulties

Behaviour Can Change Programme

Isabella's nursery

Practitioners can do a lot to create a space and climate that fosters good behaviour in every sense. The features of the physical environment, such as the size and layout, colours and lighting, and temperature of an area can have an effect upon everyone's mood and the way in which children behave. For example, a large, cold, echoing hall encourages children of all ages to run around: it offers an invitation for children and adults to raise their voices and is not conducive to settling down to any type of learning activity. By using screens and furniture to divide the space available into specific areas such as a book area, quiet drawing area, home corner, large play and sand/water tray areas, you can create a more secure and comfortable environment. The use of soft furnishings such as mats, cushions, curtains and wall displays will help to absorb sound in an otherwise noisy hall as well as making it more cosy and inviting.

The space

- If the hall/room is very large, think about creating different areas for different activities. Use screens, curtains, furniture, plants and shelving to divide a large space into more cosy areas where children feel secure.
- Try to provide some quiet areas that are sectioned off from the noisier activities to encourage appropriate behaviours for various activities and reduce distraction for the child who is sharing a book, concentrating on a matching activity or listening to a tape. Identify a 'time out' spot.
- Make sure children can move freely between furniture/displays at appropriate speeds and without invading the personal space of others.
- Provide adequate storage for coats and other belongings and ensure that the children know where this is – some children panic if they don't know where their things are. A supply of clothes pegs to keep hats, coats and gloves together may be one way of preventing lost property problems. Simple shoe bags are also

useful to keep not only both shoes but also other small items of clothing together. Ask parents/carers to make these, or enlist the help of someone with a sewing machine to make a 'job lot' for the group (curtains/bed

linen from charity shops will provide cheap material). Getting children used to looking after their belongings will be valuable training for 'big school'.

- Label everything with words and pictures.
- Make sure that storage is at child height and that everyday items, such as pencils, paper and crayons, are accessible so that the children can organize their own equipment.
- Think carefully about ventilation. Is enough fresh air available? Can windows be opened safely on a hot day?
- Lighting can have a big effect on mood and concentration. Natural light is best, but where artificial lighting is needed, try to ensure that this is as 'natural' as possible and adequate for the tasks undertaken. Good lighting will be especially important for children with visual impairment.
- Temperature is an important factor in feeling comfortable (and amenable!) – even adults are more likely to be irritable and tetchy if they are hot and bothered, thirsty and lethargic. Try to maintain an even temperature in the setting and help parents/carers to provide suitable clothing by suggesting a layered style of dress – T-shirt under sweater or sweatshirt, under coat – to allow children to peel off when they get hot. Keep a box of spare clothing – parents/carers are usually happy to donate outgrown items. In cold weather, encourage warm clothing and build in regular exercise/movement activities rather than relying on high-setting heating.
- Security is important; ensure that children can't leave the room/building on their own – is it possible to fit high door handles?
- Display general information (holiday dates, etc.) on a noticeboard, but back up with verbal reminders – not all adults can or do read notices.

Display and learning resources

- There should be a visual timetable of the day positioned at child height – use pictures and/or photographs and arrows to show sequence. Involve the children in the discussion about the structure of the day by asking them to find the appropriate picture of activities to put up on the board. A visual or pictorial timetable can be a simple set of photos or pictures of the activities of the day. These could be laminated and stuck to a child-height board (by using Velcro on the back) or hung on a line every morning with the help of the children. This visual reminder of the session helps to give structure to the child with difficulties and is good for all children. When changes to the routine are planned this will help to warn children in a very clear way about what will happen.

- A box of visual aids should be kept ready for instruction times to accompany talk/discussions.
- Have clearly visible rules on display with accompanying pictures.
- Display the children's work as professionally as you can, thereby placing instant value on their efforts.
- Choose easy-to-put-on aprons so that children are encouraged to get themselves ready for painting/water play activities.

Tiger by Gabriel

Rooster by Gabriel

Managing staff

Having created an early years setting that has all the physical features of a calm, comfortable and welcoming learning environment, how do you keep it that way?

How practitioners work together and manage the children in their care strongly affects the way those children feel and behave. For example, if it is the usual policy for adults to talk to each other using raised voices, or to shout across to the person on the other side of the room, it is hardly surprising if the children do the same. Providing good role models in the way you behave and the way in which you talk to both adults and children are vital parts of your management strategy.

The role of the teaching assistant

The role of the teaching assistant is becoming increasingly complex. Depending upon how schools manage their inclusion systems, it can be that teaching assistants are more and more involved in the support of children with additional needs.

Key areas for the teaching assistant:

- preparing materials for activities and tasks;
- helping children to participate;
- helping children to be independent;
- supporting individual children;
- supporting the teacher;
- supporting the curriculum;
- supporting the school;
- working with outside agencies;
- assisting with physical needs;

- modelling good practice;
- freeing up the teacher to teach smaller groups;
- providing feedback;
- helping to raise standards;
- identifying early signs of disruptive behaviours.

Inclusion managers give much consideration to the training needs of staff, and many teaching assistants have become experienced at identifying needs and assisting with meeting these.

Behavioural difficulties are associated with a range of additional or special educational needs. In the very young child, perhaps attending a large foundation unit, consideration will need to be given to the physical environment, to groupings, to strategies for meeting needs. Behavioural difficulties arise out of complex situations, and careful consideration will need to be applied to the identification of special needs and to meeting these.

Large foundation units with perhaps over 100 children may represent a difficult environment for a child with behavioural difficulties. Awareness about the types of behaviour being demonstrated and recording these in observations are important for future planning. Teaching assistants should be trained in observing in a range of contexts and in objective recording.

Visual representations of basic rules, visual timetables and clear visual aids for key points of reference should be clearly displayed for the whole group. Teaching assistants will need to identify those children with additional needs in whole-group situations so that individual support can be offered in terms of assisting attention and listening, and reinforcing language. Children with difficulties should be seated towards the front of the group and to one side.

For instructions given to the whole group a similar approach may be required in addition to behaviour modelling. For example, when a set of instructions is issued, the teaching assistant may break these down into simple, clear instructions, one at a time and accompanied with modelling or visual aid if necessary.

For unstructured times of the day, e.g. transition from one place to another, tidy up or snack, there will need to be extra support in terms of a 'structure' that can be relied upon for most situations. For play times or outdoor sessions, some children will require a personal plan and perhaps a buddy system, place of refuge, set activities or the opportunity to withdraw.

Teaching assistants should give due consideration to the language they use to address children with behaviour and or language-processing difficulties. In general, reduced language – key words – should be used, especially when trying to get a child to comply or when giving instructions. Lengthy explanations should be avoided.

Unacceptable behaviours should not be ignored but should be dealt with swiftly in accordance with the behaviour policy of the school. Behaviours that are not causing harm to others, e.g. going under the table, refusing to take a hat off, etc., should probably be ignored since to highlight these can result in even greater 'offending'. Obsessive behaviours should be ignored if they are not having a significant impact upon the child's ability to take part in activities or to make progress. Some children can be quite easily distracted from repetitive actions and can be encouraged to take part in a task or activity. If behaviours such as repetition or obsession take over a child's time completely, discussions should take place about how to address these. The involvement of other professionals may be sought in the first instance in order to establish what the causes are.

For children with significant behavioural difficulties, teaching assistants may be required to record behaviour. Any recording should be factual, objective and should include the antecedent, the behaviour and the consequence.

Communicating

- Use a calm, clear, unhurried voice.
- Be assertive and 'tell' children what you would like them to do – a legitimate response to a question such as 'Would you like to sit here?' is 'No.' It is better to say 'I would like you to sit on the carpet.'
- Do not talk about children or their families while they can overhear you unless it is to praise them. If possible, provide somewhere discreet for parents/carers to talk to you in private.
- Before every session make expectations about behaviour very clear (use positive language, e.g. 'speak quietly').
- Use simple instructions, one or two at a time, e.g. 'Hang your coat up' rather than 'Hang your coat up, take your name card, put it in the box and then sit on the carpet.' When the child has completed one task, then give the next instruction.
- Do not assume that all children have understood what to do. Some are very adept at disguising the fact that they do not understand every word spoken. Check understanding – 'Darren, can you remember two things I said about playing in the water? . . . Who can help him out?'
- Make children aware of the consequences of breaking the rules: 'I hope everyone will sit still and listen to the story. If anyone starts shouting out or moving around, they will be spoiling the story for everyone else. Mrs Hopkins will take them to the time out corner and they won't find out what happens to Harry in the story.'

General good practice strategies

- Give one member of your staff the responsibility of meeting and greeting every child and adult each day on a rota system. This can help to create good working relationships with parents/carers and provide an opportunity for passing on information.
- During adult-adult interaction, model appropriate behaviours such as being polite, patient, understanding, etc.
- Always model the expected behaviours, for example saying 'thank you' when given a drink or biscuit or asking a child, 'May I share that toy with you?'
- Let off steam only when the children are gone – unless you can provide a good model for managing stress! 'Oh dear! This stapler keeps going wrong and I'm getting into a temper with it. I'm going to put it down now and try it again later.'
- Appoint a trusted adult for a particular child to go to for support when he is feeling anxious or angry.

- Use group/circle times to discuss any issues relating to behaviour in an anonymous manner. Use characters in stories or puppets. Always bear in mind that some children do not like speaking in front of groups of people – that preference ought to be respected.
- Use a device such as a rain stick to gain attention without having to raise your voice – a child could be responsible for shaking this when you give a sign.
- Have a puppet which goes into 'hiding' if it gets too noisy.
- Have rewards ready for appropriate behaviours and give them out instantly.
- Ignore any inappropriate behaviours (health and safety permitting) and praise the other children who are behaving well.
- Employ a buddy system if children are old or mature enough to gain from this role modelling. This is where a mature, well-behaved child is paired up with a child who will benefit from his positive influence.
- Use a home-school contact book that contains positive comments so that parents/ carers and pre-school staff can highlight the 'good' rather than dwell on the negative.
- Try not to use story time as a 'tidy up' time for other staff or as a time for putting up displays. This provides an alternative focus of attention for the children.
- Structure the day so that children are not expected to sit for long periods on hard flooring (try this yourself – it doesn't take long to become uncomfortable on some surfaces).
- Be prepared to abandon some activities if they are causing unexpected results – even (or especially) if an Ofsted inspector is present!
- Make sure activities are appropriate and that interest levels are high. For example, make sure that activities provide direct experiences: 'doing' helps the learning process. Ensure that children can identify with topics by relating them to their own experiences so that they are more meaningful. This will maximize curiosity levels and hopefully minimize off-task behaviours.
- Anticipate behaviours – intervene quickly at the early stages of problematic behaviours.
- Recognize achievements and make positive comments, e.g. 'You must be really pleased with that painting, I see that you have really tried hard to use all the colours on the table.'
- Remove items causing inappropriate behaviours.

Strategies for children with behavioural difficulties

Visual timetable of the session

This will need to be broken down into manageable 'chunks' depending upon the age and development of the child.

A visual timetable can be used at home as well as in an educational setting. Some children may require sequential pictures of everyday events, for example the sequence of dressing, washing, brushing teeth, bathing, etc. Simple line drawings are best. For easy use, a laminated base with Velcro squares is advisable. Pictures of events can easily be stuck onto the base and changed when necessary. The child should be involved in placing the pictures. Changes to the timetable should be included and frequent verbal reminders about the change should be employed.

Visual aids

Children with behavioural difficulties benefit from a high degree of visual aid to accompany speech. The aids should be as simple as possible – simple black line drawings on white card work well. Sequential pictures for everyday events and routines are useful.

Choice making

Children with difficulties require simple choices at first. Adults should offer a maximum of two things to choose from and gradually extend these according to the developmental level of the child.

Behaviour plan

Settings should draw up behaviour plans for children with behavioural difficulties. This should be drawn up with parental consent and input. The plan should highlight how staff will respond to behaviours so that consistency can be maintained; for example how staff will handle aggression, swearing, running away, etc. Sanctions and rewards should be outlined. The plan can be carried over into the home for consistency, but ALL family members would need to stick to it to have maximum impact.

Visual rules

All settings should have a set of visual rules on display. They need to be very simple and easily remembered. Individual children should be reminded upon entry to the setting what the rules are, and should be encouraged to see themselves as responsible for their own behaviour. If the rules are broken, staff should avoid lengthy explanations and stick to the points on the behaviour plan/visual rules.

Good sitting, good looking, good listening

Settings should consider visual methods of reminding children of expected or wanted behaviours, and simple visual cue cards are a successful way of achieving this.

Stop sign

A universal 'stop' sign can be very useful for children who have difficulty responding to 'No.'

Stop, look and listen

A visual sign for gaining attention is useful when children are engaging in disruptive behaviour or are becoming excitable.

Time out

If possible, time out should only be used for short periods (as a general rule, one minute for every year of the child's age). The place in which time out is used should be free of stimuli; adults should give no attention, either negative or positive, and no eye contact.

Sanctuary

A place of sanctuary may be beneficial. This could be a screened area, a tent or den or simply a bean bag.

Home-school liaison books

A book that goes back and forth between home and school is useful for raising self-esteem. The book should contain positive comments only and possibly things/ activities/achievements that can be shared.

Responsibility

Give children responsibility. For example, depending upon the age and developmental level of children, they can be 'helper' for the day, be responsible for tidying up, run errands for adults, be responsible for an area of the nursery/school, help at snack times. Responsibility raises self-esteem.

Exit cards

Depending upon routines and staffing, exit cards are a way of giving children the choice of going into another room or place in the setting via the use of a known system.

Rewards

Reward wanted behaviours every time at first. Reward realistically; for example use praise, tokens, time with a favourite activity or toy.

Use of names

Use a child's name when highlighting wanted behaviours. Try to avoid using their name when noticing negative behaviours.

Behaviour Can Change Programme

A behaviour management plan is a working strategy that is devised in partnership with parents/carers. This plan describes strategies that will be employed by all staff working with the child. It may also outline some aims for the parents/carers and the child herself on which to work. The plan/programme is regularly evaluated and updated and provides evidence that a number of strategies have been planned and implemented before seeking further advice. Remember, some children need longer 'settling in' periods, and differentiating like this may meet the child's needs without necessarily taking the SEN (Special Educational Needs) route. There is an example format of a behaviour management programme below.

Behaviour Can Change Programme

Name of child

_____

List of strengths

_____

List of difficulties

_____

Priority difficulty

_____

Desired outcome

_____

Strategy to be used

_____

How will the child be rewarded?

_____

What to do if behaviour occurs

_____

How will the behaviour be recorded?

_____

Date Started _____   Signed _____

Date of Review _____

SECTION 5

Technology in the early years

Using technology with children

Using technology for communication with parents and carers

Technology guidelines for staff

Technology is here to stay, whether we are happy with it or not. The use of tablets and mobile phones is the subject of much debate in the press and there is a lot of conflicting information around, which makes it difficult for those in charge of setting the curriculum of a pre-school to make a decision on the priority and place of technology in their own establishment. Recent research suggests that, for instance, two children sharing the use of a tablet to play a game or do a puzzle results in measurable and positive benefits. On the other hand, others in the technology industry fear that over-reliance on small screen gadgets is having a detrimental effect on children's ability to communicate effectively in the 'real' world, and others have raised concerns regarding eyesight and the poor posture of youngsters as they pore over their gadgets.

Many experienced staff who work with young children are genuinely concerned that all too often pupils arrive in the pre-school with limited communication and language skills and feel that the over-reliance of parents on their mobile device are depriving their offspring of quality face-to-face interaction. Certainly, nothing looks sadder than a parent hunched over their mobile phone, pushing a forward-facing stroller with one hand while texting with the other as their child stares off into space. Missing these crucial one-to-one times can, it is feared, deprive very young children of the opportunity to experience the cadences of speech and the accompanying facial expressions and turn-taking which increases a youngster's ability to communicate with the world at large. One only has to observe some families eating out to realize that they might just as well be eating out individually because everyone is peering at their mobile device throughout the meal rather than talking with each other. Arriving in a pre-school setting without the requisite experience and knowledge of how to interact successfully with adults and children can put a youngster at a serious disadvantage right at the start of their education and may have repercussions in the future.

While some children may well have been over-exposed to electronic gadgetry and will be very adept at manipulating the icons on a tablet, be able to switch things on and off, start again, expand and contract pictures on the touchscreen, swipe the pages on an e-book and dart from one activity to another, there may well be others who have had no experience of technology at all. Children today will have to learn to be familiar with technology as they work their way through the education system. Primary and secondary schools vary wildly in their use of tablets during the school day – some only using them for administration purposes, setting homework and assessment recording, while other establishments use tablets throughout the school day. The early years settings, therefore, have a responsibility to ensure that all the children in their care are well equipped to deal with the use of technology, whatever their out-of-school experience may be.

Isabella

Using technology with children

Those in charge of the setting will have to make a decision on how and when to use electronic gadgets. Deciding on whether to make the use of tablet devices, set up with age-appropriate puzzles or games, as part of the general daily routine or as an occasional activity for the children is a matter of choice for the management and staff who organize and manage the curriculum. Electronic devices are expensive pieces of equipment and do not always sit comfortably alongside paint, glue or sand and water play and may therefore need closer supervision throughout the school day than staffing numbers will comfortably allow. Children who are allowed free access to devices at home may be very adept at finding unsuitable games or cartoons to watch and care needs to be taken to ensure that only appropriate items are available in the setting. Any device used by the children will need to be exclusively set up for that purpose. Time-limiting the use of electronic devices may be the only way to ensure that only appropriate activities are in use and a count-down timer on the screen coupled with a conventional clock/timer will help to prevent some youngsters staying glued to the device for too long.

There are many interesting and colourful games and puzzles available for a pre-school setting to purchase or download but these will need to be selected with care. It is well known that boys in particular can be reluctant writers, especially those who favour their left hand, and it is important that early years settings do not inadvertently reinforce the use of touchscreens over the use of conventional mark-making items. There are some very tempting letter formation and early writing programmes which demonstrate directionality in a colourful and entertaining way. These are excellent for demonstrating the way letters are formed but if the children are just allowed to trace over the shapes on the screen, they do not always develop the necessary finger strength to hold a pencil or crayon with a tripod grip, although some manufacturers are taking steps to address this.

Providing plenty of activities that do encourage fine motor control and manual dexterity, such as construction toys, play dough and threading, may need to be promoted to ensure that children do develop the necessary skills. The early years setting should offer a range of 'old fashioned' board games and pencil and paper games to encourage manual dexterity, including simple jigsaws, dominoes, matching games, picture bingo, snakes and ladders or marble rolling activities to give children concrete experience of playing with others. Colourful construction bricks and toys need to be available at all times to encourage co-operative and inventive play. In many households there is a preference for the 'clean and tidy' use of a tablet over the undoubtedly messy and hazardous plastic brick! Children need to experience the effort of constructing a large and elaborate edifice (and learn how to tidy up) as well as being confident with how the pages of a printed book 'work'.

Using technology for communication with parents and carers

Of course it is expected that information, updates and reminders will be communicated via texts to parents and carers. However, a paper copy of, for instance, school closures, term dates and holidays, visits from the photographer and other events should always be available and on display. Mobile phones can run out of credit, get lost, forgotten, stolen or are just unreliable and there is no substitute for a member of staff being on duty at the door on arrival and departure to remind parents of important information and upcoming events. Not all parents are comfortable with the 'school gate chat' whereby information is disseminated amongst the parents and carers while waiting for their offspring to emerge from the pre-school. Many parents arrive by car and often at the last minute, thereby avoiding vital information exchange opportunities. The setting should, therefore, be very clear about how technology will be used and be consistent in how they do it. Many pre-school settings find it useful to appoint a member of staff who is both comfortable and adept with technology to be the co-ordinator who takes responsibility for monitoring what and when activities are available and who will keep up to date on available research from organizations such as the Centre for Research in Digital Education.

Technology guidelines for staff

Aside from the use of technology by the children themselves and to keep parents informed, a strictly adhered to policy of its use by staff working in the setting needs to be in place. Obviously the photographing of children is a safeguarding issue and a clear policy should be in place so that privacy is preserved for both adults and children. Staff, parents and carers need to be made aware that the pre-school setting is not somewhere for mobile phones and social media to be in use and that identity and security have to be a priority. Staff may need to be reminded that only devices which are specifically provided for the children to use are accessible and private phones or tablets should not be in evidence during the working day. It is not safe to assume that all adults working with the children are fully aware of the repercussions of using their own personal devices inadvertently or inappropriately. Regular updating of safeguarding training will go some way to ensure that all staff remain conscious of the importance of using technology wisely. Management will need to ensure that their policy on the use of technology by children and staff is kept up to date and readily available so that parents are well-informed and reassured.

SECTION 6

Moving on
Transition to school

Providing information

Managing anxiety

Making transition easier

Children who have started at pre-school at the same time and have stayed together throughout their early years do not necessarily move on to a mainstream school at the same time and some parents and carers (and children) find this very confusing. Currently in the UK it is compulsory for children to start school at the beginning of the term following their fifth birthday although schools are required to provide education from 1 September following the child's fourth birthday. Many children are more than ready to start in the mainstream setting at the earliest opportunity.

Providing information

By referring parents/carers to reliable, timely and accurate information, the pre-school setting will help parents to make an informed choice, and to avoid disappointment and missed deadlines. A quick glance at the www.gov.uk website and selection of the appropriate postcode will lead to a wealth of general information, but this may not be easy for parents/carers to navigate if they are new to an area or new to the process. In some areas of the UK the choice is wide and confusing and may include reference to:

- Infant/Junior/Primary schools;
- Community schools (usually run by the local authority);
- Foundation/Voluntary/Faith/Free schools;
- Academies (run by a governing body and independent of the local authority) maybe with links to other schools further afield;
- Independent/Private schools/Prep schools/Public schools (fee paying);
- Special schools for children with additional needs;
- Middle schools (some areas);
- High schools;
- Comprehensive schools;
- Grammar schools (in some areas), which use a selective examination process often at the age of 11;
- Sixth Form Colleges.

When faced with such a list, some parents/carers will become anxious that they may not choose the 'right' school for their child. Coupled with the fact that some parents/carers are restricted by lack of transport or time to get to the mainstream school of their choice it may be difficult to advise everyone appropriately but signposting them in plenty of time will do much to alleviate problems.

It is important that the pre-school setting maintains an informed, professional (but neutral) stance on the subject of choosing and starting school and is prepared to signpost parents in the right direction without influencing decisions, which must be made by the parents/carers themselves. By providing accurate and timely information, the pre-school can help to reduce unnecessary angst and thereby minimize the risk of the children picking up any anxious vibes from home. Those in charge of the pre-school will need to have accurate information about the local process for starting mainstream school, be alert to changes in procedures and ensure that staff give unbiased and accurate information.

Local authorities maintain up-to-date information on their websites but staff in the pre-school setting are in a unique position to identify and help those parents who may need extra help. Parents/carers who have had experience of older children in the family moving on seamlessly to their nearest local primary school and onwards and upwards through the education system, may be completely unaware that local procedures and choices have changed a great deal in the intervening years, and alerting them to the current practice may need extra consideration. Parents/carers who have limited educational backgrounds themselves or do not have English as their first language may need support to ensure that they follow the correct procedures for applying for mainstream school places. Many will assume that if the pre-school is actually on the same site as the school, then a place is automatically available without any active input, and will need to be reminded to apply for a place at the chosen school. For the most part, application for school places has to be completed online, which is not always easy if using the small screen on a mobile phone. Pre-schools can help to make applications easier if a device with a large screen is available for parental use.

Most good pre-school settings have noted and recorded a great deal of useful information about the children in their care and if these have been shared regularly with the parents/carers they will be in a good position to know what to look for in a school to provide the right setting for their child. Although 'parental choice' is the key principle, some parents find this very hard. Some mainstream schools are very pro-active at promoting their intake procedures with open days, information evenings and glossy brochures, etc. and if the pre-school makes dates and times available through their noticeboard, e-mails and newsletters this will enable as many parents as possible to be aware of what they need to do. Pre-schools should also have copies of any booklets or other information that local schools provide so that parents who are not so pro-active are aware of what is available.

Some pre-schools are happy to provide the venue for information meetings so that schools and local authorities can explain their transition procedures or distribute their hard copy information. It may be worthwhile inviting the Special Needs Coordinators from local schools in to see the setting in action and give any interested parents the opportunity to ask general questions.

Managing anxiety

When children come to the natural end of their time in pre-school several issues come to the forefront and parents frequently become quite anxious about the next step, especially if the child is their first offspring to move on to 'big school'. Staff in the pre-school will need to be alert to those youngsters who are picking up on the adults' uncertainties and may need to give some children extra reassurance and time to talk. It is not unusual for children, who might be particularly anxious about the next step, to revert to more immature behaviour such as playing with toys which they had previously outgrown or to become very clingy with adults at home and in the setting. Some youngsters seem to sense that change is on the horizon and think that, by reverting to the behaviour of younger children, they can fend off the inevitable and be allowed to stay on in the security of the pre-school setting. Several publishers produce books about starting 'Big School' or making new friends and a selection of suitable titles readily available and prominently displayed in the early years setting may encourage parents to think about the next step in a positive way.

In some parts of the country, where places at the most popular schools are at a premium, parents are sometimes faced with an intimidating amount of information, deadlines and, unfortunately, school-gate gossip, which increases their concern about the next step. However, parents and carers vary a great deal in how they approach the process, with some reading every Ofsted report available, arranging visits and scouring the internet for all available information, while others just assume that a place will be readily available at the nearest school to home. With the introduction of free schools in some areas, primary schools becoming academies and being linked with other schools as part of a geographically diverse consortium, oversubscription of popular schools and the possible added complication of eleven plus selection looming in the future in some local authority areas, some families are understandably confused and anxious.

Children who live in split households, possibly spending weekends and weekdays in different locations, may be particularly worried about transition to a new educational setting. If staff in the pre-school are aware that parents are having difficulty sorting out a mutually acceptable, or convenient, school and especially if they have noticed a change in the child's behaviour and if the child has been acting out in some way, it may be possible to set up a meeting to help sort matters out. Choice of school has to be the parents' decision, but impartial advice and letting parents know the effect on their child of being unsure where they will be going after pre-school ends, may make a workable compromise easier to achieve.

Cultural and social expectations may also have an influence on how a child deals with transition to the next phase and staff will need to be alert to inaccurate perceptions around, for instance, strict discipline in Key Stage 1, having to 'sit still all day' or having 'loads' of homework. The conversations overheard from much older brothers and sisters sometimes get misconstrued, and the anxious four year old may pick up unrealistic expectations of lots of writing and no toys or play times. Encouraging visits to the Reception class and getting the lie of the land (e.g. knowing where the toilets are and where they are going to eat) will do a lot to reassure the under-confident youngster.

Many pre-schools also provide 'ready for school' checklists and tips to make transition to the next phase as easy as possible. The Social and Emotional Development Checklist in Appendix 1 to this book could also be helpful for parents, as well as a display of Key Stage 1 workbooks (many of which are readily available in supermarkets), which may encourage parents to make sure their child does not find the next phase too daunting. If parents look up information on starting school on the internet and look at any parental forum they will be overwhelmed by the amount of uniform checklists and literacy and numeracy readiness instructions which pop up. Staff in the pre-school setting can do much to alleviate worries and concerns by keeping information straightforward and practical.

Making transition easier

- Set up informal and formal liaison arrangements with all the local schools that your setting 'feeds' and get to know the Key Stage 1 staff and the Special Needs Co-ordinators.
- Make sure you have the latest version of booklets and information from the Local Authority in hard copy and online form readily available for parents/carers to access.
- If possible, make visits to the mainstream school with the children who are moving on and give them opportunities to talk about it afterwards.
- Ensure you have parental consent before forwarding SEN (Special Educational Needs) records.
- Ensure all staff maintain a professional distance and allow parents/carers to make their own, well-informed, decisions.
- Remember that most children settle down happily into their new school with ease, even those who have needed considerable support throughout their pre-schooling.

Child protection, safeguarding and safer recruitment

Safeguarding

Safer recruitment and staff training

Health and safety

Staff responsibility

Case study: Danny

Creating and maintaining a professional and positive working relationship with parents and carers is essential for easing the transition of children into the pre-school setting and maintaining a confidential and collaborative approach to the child's welfare throughout their placement is an important part of the relationship. Parents need to have confidence in the well-being of their child whilst in the care of the setting and this will help to create a well-adjusted and relaxed child who will move on smoothly to the next phase of their education. Parents and carers need to feel reassured that the setting is a safe and secure place for their children to spend their days and the parents themselves need to feel listened to and that their concerns are treated with respect.

Isabella's friends in her nursery

Safeguarding

High-profile cases hitting the headlines have increased public awareness of the vulnerability of young children, and the management of early years setting must make safeguarding, in all its aspects, a priority when arranging training programmes for all their staff. The implementation of a rigorously followed Safeguarding Policy with an emphasis on accurate record-keeping and well-trained, vigilant personnel will help to reassure anxious parents that the setting they have chosen will have their child's welfare at heart. Ways of demonstrating that your setting is making safeguarding, in its widest sense, a priority might include:

- Providing parents and carers with a copy of the Safeguarding Policy when they apply to have their child admitted to the pre-school setting.
- Regularly updating and revising the policy, if necessary, and re-issuing it.
- Clear signage in the reception area, informing parents and visitors of the name of the Designated Safeguarding Lead for the establishment.
- Providing a clear display of literature on a range of related topics. This should include the NSPCC and Childline, domestic violence helplines, healthy eating, safety in the sun, the use of technology, social media and mobile phones, etc.
- Having a rigorous system of identifying visitors to the building, including signing in and out.
- Using badges for all visitors.
- Displaying the rules of the establishment simply and clearly.
- Clear identification of the First Aiders.
- Adopting a strict Recruitment Policy.
- Maintaining a clean and tidy premises.

Safer recruitment and staff training

The management of the setting should ensure that their recruitment of suitable staff follows agreed guidelines and that the setting applies a strict 'Safer Recruitment' policy. This must include, for instance, the scrupulous checking of references, using a standard application form, and checking their accuracy. The days of personal recommendation and ad hoc appointments are long gone. Any gaps in employment history need to be investigated, and checking suitability through the Disclosure and Barring Service (DBS) mechanism must be carried out before anyone is allowed to begin work, paid or unpaid.

Keeping all staff up to date with regular child protection and safeguarding courses, through the NSPCC or the local authority, will ensure, as far as possible, that everyone employed by the setting, including administrative staff and caretakers, is fully aware of their responsibilities.

Health and safety

Management obviously need to examine their premises and equipment regularly for 'health and safety'. The term 'health and safety' often produces groans and raised eyebrows, implying interference and over-the-top restrictions, but when young children who have not developed an awareness of their own risk are involved, it is vital that they are fully protected from harm in its widest sense. No establishment wants to be the subject of an article in the local press entitled 'Toddler finds his own way home when left alone in the playground!'

Premises obviously need to be clean, free from physical dangers, with adequate lighting, toilet facilities, secure entrances and exits, etc. Safe working practices and appropriate staff behaviour also need constant vigilance by all.

Staff responsibility

The manner in which members of staff address one another and the children needs to be carefully observed and instances of inappropriate comments should be swiftly addressed. Good role models will encourage good behaviour and positive relationships throughout the setting. A happy and secure staff team, who have confidence in their managers, will feel able to report any concerns, knowing they will be listened to and their issues followed up. This in turn will go a long way towards creating an emotionally stable and harmonious atmosphere and will reassure parents and carers that their child is in safe and caring hands.

It is a sad fact that some children do live in circumstances that are far from ideal. Families who move house frequently and do not appear to have a supportive network of family and friends may be particularly prone to living with stress, and may show indications that cause staff to be extra vigilant for signs that the children need extra support. If staff do observe behaviour or physical signs that cause concern, it is important that these are accurately recorded and processed in accordance with the Safeguarding Policy. The senior member of staff with designated responsibility for safeguarding needs to ensure that all staff and any volunteers are fully aware of how child protection concerns must be managed. Confidentiality needs to be maintained but, at the same time, the safety of the child is paramount. All staff, whatever their role, need to be aware of their responsibility to record and report any issues in the correct way.

The early years setting may well be the first time that children have socialized outside the home and it may also be the first time that the parent/carer has been able to meet with others outside the immediate family. It is, therefore, quite possible that a member of staff will be the first person who becomes aware of difficulties that the family are experiencing – financial, emotional or physical – and they need to be trained and ready to know how to respond appropriately and be able to signpost or alert the correct organization. The noticeboard of the setting can be a discreet and useful place to display details of contact lines and help centres – those who are aware that they need to get some advice will be able to take down the relevant numbers directly into their mobile phone without being observed picking up specific literature. There is a wealth of publications around which could be included in a small lending library. Early years settings that share premises with, for instance, schools or health centres, will be in a good position to combine resources. Settings can also obtain free literature from a wide range of organizations and agencies, including the NSPCC, Childline, Healthy Schools, the NHS and local safeguarding networks. It is quite likely that parents and carers themselves may have access to information that could usefully be made available to the setting. If at all possible, a private office where personal matters may be aired confidentially should be made available.

Nursery setting by Eden

CASE STUDY

Danny

Danny has recently started at the pre-school and is brought in promptly each day by both his mother and father. He is a polite boy and the parents seem to be happy with the setting, and he leaves them quite happily. Once his parents leave the premises Danny initially plays contentedly with the activity to which he has been taken. However, when he is later given a choice of activity to play with, Danny becomes very confused, sometimes just curling up in a ball on a cushion in the book corner, but more recently he has begun to rush around the setting without stopping, grabbing items from each area and dropping them anywhere. He rejects efforts by the staff to calm him down and settle to an activity. He eventually tires himself out and goes and lies down on the cushions. He leaves with his mother at the end of the session without difficulty but always appears subdued.

Staff were concerned that these outbursts occurred on a daily basis and there appeared to be no consoling or distracting him. The Head of the pre-school asked Danny's mother to come into the setting at the end of the session to discuss his behaviour. His mother explained that they had moved house from another part of the country recently and were now living in an upstairs flat and Danny's father did night work, so Danny was not allowed to play with anything other than the toy that he was allowed that day. Danny's father did not like mess around the house, and this included Danny's playthings; he had decided that Danny should be allowed one quiet toy a day to keep the noise down and the house tidy. Staff realized that their more relaxed attitude to children's needs to play with a variety of toys and to talk, laugh and shout when appropriate was too much for Danny to handle in one go. He was not allowed choice at home or to make a noise indoors, and when presented with what appeared to be an unlimited selection of activities, he simply over-reacted. His mother also said that Danny's father did not like her to go out and about without him, so taking Danny to the park or to a children's soft play gym had not been possible. He had only agreed to Danny attending the pre-school when workmates had said that school was compulsory and Danny would be reaching school age within the next few months. She was anxious to get home as Danny's father would in all likelihood question why she was late home from picking him up. She added that he was very generous with items for the house and Danny did have some expensive (but largely unused) toys and games. The Head agreed that in the short term they would handle Danny's difficulty with moving on to further activities by guiding him to a suitable toy, and an adult would remain nearby to forestall any outbursts and reassure him that it was fine to change activities. They would monitor his ability to pick and choose toys and activities for himself and ensure that he had the opportunity to experience a wide range of age-appropriate things to do. It was agreed that Danny's mother would call in again in a week's time a few minutes before the session ended to see how he was doing.

After Danny's mother had left, the Head and two other senior members of staff met to discuss the issues raised by Danny's mother. They were concerned that not only did Danny appear to lead a restricted lifestyle at home, it was clear that his mother was not accessing the wider networks of support that young mothers frequently create for themselves. She was new to the area, did not appear to have family close by, and appeared to need to account for her whereabouts. Staff had encountered similar situations to this in the past, felt that this was potentially a very sensitive situation and were keen not to expose Danny's mother to cross-examination about any meetings or discussions. The Head suggested that she might benefit from meeting with another sympathetic parent in the pre-school whose child was due to start school soon and who could strike up at least a casual friendship. She also suggested that as there were several useful leaflets on a variety of domestic abuse situations available, they could make these available for Danny's mother to look at when she picked him up. They also agreed to place some contact cards for the local domestic abuse helpline in the ladies' toilet. The staff felt it was too soon to jump to conclusions that the family were in immediate need for a pro-active referral to, for instance, Women's Aid. However, from their experience, this family needed support, and the mother in particular needed to become more informed about what an acceptable level of independence should be. The Head agreed that careful monitoring of Danny's demeanour should be undertaken and that every opportunity should be given to the mother to raise any concerns. It was felt that any indication of a request for help from either parent or a disclosure of any kind from Danny should be responded to as a priority.

SECTION 8

The statutory process
Education and Health Care Plan

Requesting an EHC Plan

Creating an EHC Plan

Provision in the early years

The Department for Education published an Early Years guide to the 0-25 SEND (Special Educational Needs and Disability) Code of Practice in September 2014 and this is available online. We do not intend to reproduce this but refer to it.

The previous system of Statutory Assessment has been updated and replaced by the implementation of the Education and Health Care Plan (EHCP). We refer to this as EHCP or the EHC Plan. The new process attempts to make it a priority for all professionals to work more closely together in order to produce a combined EHCP that is agreed and contributed to by all concerned and puts parents and carers at the heart of the process.

The EHCP identifies children who need more support than is available through Special Educational Needs (SEN) support. The EHCP identifies educational, health and social needs and sets out the additional support to meet those needs.

Requesting an EHC Plan

A young person over the age of 16 (to 25) can ask for an assessment.

A parent/carer can ask the local authority for an assessment.

A request can be made by doctors, health visitors, teachers, parents.

If an assessment is carried out, the local authority will require:

☐ reports from your child's school, nursery, childminder;
☐ doctors' assessments;
☐ a letter from parent/carer about the child's needs.

The local authority will tell you within 16 weeks whether the EHC Plan is to be made.

Creating an EHC Plan

☐ Your local authority will send you a draft plan.
☐ You have 15 days to comment, including if you want your child to attend special provision.
☐ Your local authority has 20 weeks from the date of the assessment to give you the final EHC Plan.

Additional information is provided in the SEND Code of Practice (2014), including processes in the case of disputes and disagreements. This document can be viewed or downloaded at GOV.UK websites.

Provision in the early years

The Early Years Foundation Stage Framework (EYFS Framework) sets out requirements for supporting children with additional needs and for promoting equality.

The Framework sets out standards that all Ofsted registered providers must meet to ensure that children develop and learn well and are kept healthy and safe.

That includes ongoing assessment of progress. Early years providers should have arrangements in place that include a clear approach to assessing Special Educational Needs. Practitioners should make themselves aware of the The Equality Act of 2010, The Statutory Framework for the Early Years Foundation Stage, The Special Educational Needs and Disability Regulations 2014. At the end of the EYFS a profile of the child's knowledge, understanding and abilities will have been completed. This is particularly helpful for children with SEN and should inform planning for future learning and identify any additional needs for support.

The old approach to support for children (Action and Action Plus) have been replaced by a new system of support in the early years. All settings should adopt a graduated approach with four stages of action: assess, plan, do and review.

Assess

In cooperation with the child's parents and the setting SENCO (Special Educational Needs Coordinator), an initial assessment of need should be carried out. This should be reviewed regularly to ensure that support is matched to need. Where there is little or no progress, more specialized assessment may be carried out. Any intervention should be carried out with parental consent.

Plan

Where it is decided to provide SEN support, the practitioner and the SENCO should agree the outcomes they are seeking, the interventions and support to be put in place and the expected impact on progress, development or behaviour. A date for review should be set. Any relevant staff development needs should be identified and addressed. Parents should be consulted at every step of the process and be involved in planning support where appropriate.

Do

The early years practitioner, usually the key person, remains responsible for working with the child on a daily basis. With support from the SENCO they should oversee the implementation of the interventions/plan or programmes agreed. The SENCO should support the practitioner in assessing the child's response and advising upon the effectiveness of the implementation of support.

Review

The effectiveness of the support plan should be reviewed in line with the agreed date. Parents and practitioners should agree any changes to outcomes and support for the child.

The cycle of action should be revisited in increasing detail and frequency to identify the best way forward. Any future review meeting dates should be set and should include assessments, planning and desired outcomes.

The graduated approach should be led and co-ordinated by the setting SENCO. This should be informed by the EYSF materials, the Early Years Outcomes guidance and Early Support resources (information is available at the National Children's Bureau website).

Where a child has an EHC Plan, the local authority must review the plan every 12 months. As part of the review, the local authority can ask settings, and require maintained nursery schools, to convene and hold the annual review meeting on its behalf. Further information is available in the Code of Practice 0-25 2014, published by the Department for Education and available at GOV.UK websites.

APPENDIX 1

Social and Emotional Development Checklist

It is important that any checklist is used with sensitivity. It should not be used to highlight what the child cannot do or to create unrealistic expectations. Instead, it should be seen as a very rough guide to the developmental steps most children take between the ages of two and five.

Age two to three years

- ☐ Increasing cooperation with parental requests: will *usually* do what is asked.

- ☐ May prefer to play alongside other children rather than with them.

- ☐ Finds difficulty in taking turns and sharing.

- ☐ Needs help to resolve problems with peers, e.g. if another child will not let him play with a toy.

- ☐ Carries out simple instructions, e.g. bringing or taking objects from room to room.

- ☐ Sits with adult to share books for five minutes.

- ☐ Says 'please' and 'thank you' when reminded.

- ☐ Makes attempts to help parent/carer with chores.

- ☐ Plays 'dressing up' in adult clothes.

- ☐ Makes a choice between, e.g. a cake or a biscuit, when asked.

- ☐ Shows understanding of feeling by verbalizing, 'Maddy is hurt – she's crying.'

- ☐ Shows own feelings such as fear, affection etc.

- ☐ Beginning to respond to 'obvious' humour.

Age three to four years

☐ Sings and dances to music.

☐ Imitates other children regarding the following of rules.

☐ May become angry if things don't go his way, but beginning to control feelings – less chance of temper tantrums.

☐ Greets familiar adults without reminder.

☐ Follows rules in adult-led activity.

☐ Asks permission to use a toy being played with by another child.

☐ Increasingly says 'please' and 'thank you' without reminders.

☐ Is able to the answer the telephone and talk to a familiar person.

☐ Will take turns in a game or reaching into biscuit tin etc.

☐ Cooperates with adult requests 75% of the time.

☐ Stays in own garden/playground area.

☐ Plays near and talks with other children when engaged in own activity.

☐ Often prefers to play with others, wants to please friends.

☐ Likes to dress himself and increasingly tries to be independent.

Age four to five years

☐ Asks for help when having difficulty.

☐ Contributes to adult conversation.

☐ Repeats rhymes, songs or dances.

☐ Is able to work alone at an activity for up to 20 minutes.

☐ Will apologize without a reminder.

☐ Will take turns with an increasingly larger group of children (eight or nine).

☐ Will play cooperatively with other children, forming small groups that sometimes exclude others.

☐ Shows less physical aggression (hitting others), but uses verbal threats – 'I'll kick you, I'll tell my dad.'

☐ Beginning to understand the power of rejection – 'You can't be my friend.'

☐ May lie to avoid getting into trouble – 'It wasn't me!'

☐ Dresses and eats with minimum supervision.

☐ Engages in socially acceptable behaviour in public.

(Adapted from various sources for use with settings in Medway LEA.)

Glossary

Autistic Spectrum Disorder (ASD)	a developmental disorder that is characterized by social and communication difficulties
cognition	how a child thinks and learns
emotional development	the way a child controls and expresses his feelings
expressive language	spoken language, talking
language delay	limited and/or immature use of language
language disorder	a difficulty with the understanding of words and their use
neurological	associated with the brain and nervous system
receptive language	understanding what is said
self-esteem	the way we see ourselves – a child with high self-esteem has a positive picture of himself
social	the way a child relates to her peers and adults and how she is able to respond to systems and organization

social awareness

the ability to act in an appropriate way in different settings, e.g., organized groups such as pre-school settings

speech disorder

a difficulty with pronouncing single or combined sounds and/or sentence structure

structure

giving structure to an activity or a day's activities means planning and organizing things to good effect

APPENDIX 3

Useful addresses

Centre for Research in Digital Education
www.de.ed.ac.uk

Down's Syndrome Association
Langton Down Centre
2a Langton Park
Teddington
Middlesex TW11 9PS
Helpline: 0333 121 2300
Email: info@downs-syndrome.org.uk

Family Lives
15–17 The Broadway
Hatfield
Hertfordshire AL9 5HZ
Helpline: 0808 800 2222
www.familylives.org.uk

National Autistic Society
393 City Road
London EC1 1NG
Tel: 0207 833 2299
Helpline: 0808 800 4104
Email: nas@nas.org.uk

National Children's Bureau
115 Mare Street,
London E8 4RU
Tel: 0207 843 6000
www.ncb.org.uk

NSPCC
Helpline: 0208 800 5000
www.nspcc.org.uk

Office for Advice, Assistance, Support and Information on Special Needs (OAASIS, part of the Cambian Group)
Tel: 01590 622880
www.cambiangroup.com

Pre-School Learning Alliance
50 Featherstone Street
London EC1Y 8RT
Tel: 0207 697 2500
www.pre-school.org.uk

Pyramid Education Consultants
Lion Building
Crowhurst Road
Brighton BN1 8AF
Email: pyramiduk@pecs.com
www.pecsunitedkingdom.com

Social and Emotional Behaviour Difficulties Association (SEBDA)
c/o Goldwyn School
Great Chart
Ashford TN23 3PT
Tel: 01233 622958, option 4
Email: admin@sebda.org